OЯACULE

Also by NICOLE RAZIYA FONG

PEЯFACT

published by Talonbooks

OЯACULE

Poems

with an afterword by
Andy Martrich

Nicole Raziya Fong

Talonbooks

© 2021 Nicole Raziya Fong

All rights reserved. No part of this book may be reproduced, stored in a retrieval system, or transmitted, in any form or by any means, without the prior written consent of the publisher or a licence from Access Copyright (The Canadian Copyright Licensing Agency). For a copyright licence, visit accesscopyright.ca or call toll-free 1-800-893-5777.

Talonbooks
9259 Shaughnessy Street, Vancouver, British Columbia, Canada V6P 6R4
talonbooks.com

Talonbooks is located on xʷməθkʷəy̓əm, Sḵwx̱wú7mesh, and səl̓ilwətaʔɬ Lands.

First printing: 2021

Typeset in Arno
Printed and bound in Canada on 100% post-consumer recycled paper

Interior and cover design by Typesmith

Talonbooks acknowledges the financial support of the Canada Council for the Arts, the Government of Canada through the Canada Book Fund, and the Province of British Columbia through the British Columbia Arts Council and the Book Publishing Tax Credit.

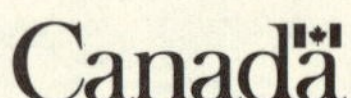

Library and Archives Canada Cataloguing in Publication

Title: ORACULE / Nicole Raziya Fong.
Names: Fong, Nicole Raziya, author.
Description: Poems. | In title, "R" in "ORACULE" appears as capitalized Cyrillic letter Ya.
Identifiers: Canadiana 20210184299 | ISBN 9781772013610 (softcover)
Classification: LCC PS8611.O5545 O73 2021 | DDC C811/.6—dc23

for Luminous

SOCRATES: Whatever is impressed upon the wax we remember and know so long as the image remains in the wax; whatever is obliterated or cannot be impressed, we forget and do not know.

THEAETETUS: Let that be our supposition.

—PLATO, *Theaetetus*
(trans. M.J. Levett, rev. Myles Burnyeat, 1990)

Dawn will soon come, weep then.

—HOMER, *The Odyssey*, book 4
(trans. Emily Wilson, 2017)

DRAMATIS PERSONAE

HEROINE
LUMINOUS – A STAR
MATERNAL LOVE
CHILD
CHORUS
ANTI-CHORUS

NOTE

Supplanted by any extant system of unveiling, the painted woman, the grotesque heroine, the dissociated child come to be cast upon an irrevocable stage. Here, the true personality begins to appear through eyes linking exterior and unseen; though it's never apparent to the outside which temporalities have begun to intersect, the spectator is always made to assume that the image presented is an entirety.

To pull an expression of seeming into encounter is to give untold life to the mask.

These songs are not meant to be sung.

This stage is not meant to be denuded.

These characters are illegitimate.

This stage is the site of an operatic voice.

This stage is the site of a silencing.

These characters are set in indecision.

These characters have unclothed.

These characters have not disrobed.

Do not sing these songs.

I

THE MEANINGLESS DIVINITY WITHIN THE FLESH THEATRE

❋ PROLOGUE DELAYING ARRIVAL INTO A SERE JUDGMENT OF FORMS ❋ A VITAL FLOWER ❋ AN INCREMENTAL EYE ❋ BY ALL CAPACITIES IT OUGHT TO HAVE BEEN ❋ THIS SAD SCATTERING OF SIGNS ❋ TO PERCEIVE INSTABILITY IN TERMS OF A FORMULAIC TOWER ❋ POINTS TOWARDS DIFFERENTIATION ❋ LATENESS (A PLATED BAUBLE) ❋ BROAD DUNES (SPARED DOWNPOUR) ❋ FORESHADOWING A GARDEN ❋ A PERCEPTIBLE FACE ❋ VISIBLE AT A DISTANCE

PROLOGUE DELAYING ARRIVAL INTO A SERE JUDGMENT OF FORMS

The performance here begins:

of sockets reduced to iterative dimension
of a well-timed cymbal crash, suggesting hilarity or catastrophe
of a blemish transposed between acts upon a previously flawless exterior
or the mourning whose evidence is concealed by a shroud
or the prayer whose veiling substantiates the backdrop to another simultaneity
only to be removed before the final scene
only again to return to the flawlessness of seeming
the perfection of the mask giving way to breath or affirmation repetitive, inseparable from life and so becoming the most evocative expression of living
or any expression of living
or any memory of living
or any dream of living you might have experienced in the past
or living in the past, unable to verify the probability of that which has already transpired
or feeling content and fulfilled in the currency of your continued life.

HEROINE and LUMINOUS stage a performance of Plato's Theaetetus, *with LUMINOUS as SOCRATES and HEROINE as THEAETETUS.*

SOCRATES
How many birds do you see there?

THEAETETUS
I am a boy whose willpower is mechanical.

SOCRATES
To accept the accordance of change is to avoid refutation.

THEAETETUS
I am a girl whose monstrosity occurs on a gradient.

SOCRATES
A pastoral throughway between change and changelessness ignites a golden chord within the skeletal system.

THEAETETUS
In a garden, on an incline.

SOCRATES
A clear, uninhabited tone.

THEAETETUS
My skin consists of a hard, colourless wax struck through with gold.
My skeletal system: soft, red honeycomb.

SOCRATES
Disparity.

THEAETETUS
This concurrence within the same name.

SOCRATES
How many birds do you see there?

THEAETETUS
An oceanic bird made of candle wax.

SOCRATES
I have been refuted.

A VITAL FLOWER

Here, an ambiguity. Here, a manner of repair whose essence is to betray vital points of tension by outlining them in ink or vermeil. Having been broken into consecutive endeavours, recombination devours essence.

Out of which HEROINE appears.

As essence might retract relative appearance from a mask, so might this likeness construct a fissure in its place. Thus, any condition that necessitates, leads to, reverses the character of the speaker in any unintended way, causing errancy to recompose the sanctity of the face.

HEROINE

I put on my face and walk out the door. I adorn myself with daylight.

LUMINOUS

(*parries an edifice*)

Enter MATERNAL LOVE.

HEROINE

(*shining her hair with a sterling silver boar-bristle brush*) I'm in a film where my distaste is heroic. Here, I'm a suffering dress, a legible hem, a dated resemblance. Here, I'm gargling a feverish whisky. I'm brushing my hair. I'm recombining a torn dress. I'm signing myself onto a page. I'm exiting the bedroom, I'm entering a waterway, et cetera, et cetera, et cetera –

MATERNAL LOVE

I'd forgotten that I needed to return your face.

MATERNAL LOVE takes the hairbrush from HEROINE and begins shining her hair.

Exit MATERNAL LOVE.

CHILD

That the room of your abjection already exists –

HEROINE

(*interjecting*) Somewhere ...

CHILD
Whether it has occurred, or is occurring –

HEROINE
(*interjecting*) If momentary, has yet to be ...

LUMINOUS
(*representing "her"*)

Enter MATERNAL LOVE.

CHILD
Failed durations of memory open their doors and close them – open them and close them –

HEROINE
Open them and close them with the faded precision of moons risen inadequately over the hills –

CHILD
(*interrupting, imitating*) "Over the hills by which we cast our equally imperfect light."

HEROINE
This light which is our currency.

MATERNAL LOVE
Any bend intended for reverence –

CHILD
(*interrupting, imitating*) "Any intended future."

LUMINOUS
(*displays an artifact*)

Exit MATERNAL LOVE.

HEROINE
Why won't you print me in your discourse?

LUMINOUS
(*stills*)

CHILD
(*despairingly*) I want to exit this fateful cinema.

AN INCREMENTAL EYE

Back then, I wrote to illusion.

Back then, truth was unveiled to be a shimmering garment, sequined with ashes.
Truth was unveiled to be an agent of distaste, dressed immaculately in echo.

This cloudy, perceptual fold encountered in the midst of illuminated night
(remembered, without naïveté) …

ANTI-CHORUS (*amorously*)

A
completion of
Who is

breeze ruins the
the image.
the actress?

Is acting?

CHORUS

I leave
upon the

my inevitable mark
stage.

So
deface the

of this

might a river
originary desert
and bulging extremity
woundedness.

So I might
an interior …
marred.

wake anew

Like the late leaves requiring
I wrote to you across a subjectless inquiry

The nature of the inquiry was to establish
any sensorium of cohesion
by which an unbreakable "line"
of experience

Might remain equally unquestioned

A breeze ruins the completion of the image
I leave my incomprehension upon the stage
So might a river deface the originary desert
and bulging extremity of this
woundedness

Like the late noon requiring
division of feature from form

CHORUS

ANTI-CHORUS

I wake anew
in the interior

Had the provocation of a moment allowed
my entrance, I might have ushered you in
behind

I might have asked

Had a moment allowed

BY ALL CAPACITIES IT OUGHT TO HAVE BEEN

HEROINE isn't what you think.
It isn't who you think it is.
If you identify with HEROINE, this perceived similarity is coincidental.
It isn't you. It isn't your mother. It isn't even me.
HEROINE is the explanation.

Please see the flashing of the light as emotive evidence. Please factor the cast of the sky's indifference into probability.

HEROINE

Very early on in the performance, I caught on to the "great deception": a pigeon on the balcony, outlined in transparency against a brick wall which related the substance of a sequined dress to the sexuality of the wearer in a way which removed any kind of precedent from the gaze's originary signing.

LUMINOUS

(*emotes in resinous gradation*)

CHILD

(*becoming audible mid-sentence*) … movement within the dream, the vehemence with which she moved each item that appeared, scattered across the floor, into a paper bag she'd then been grasping with conviction.

LUMINOUS

If woman, but not her, but –

HEROINE

The opposition between a past which occurred, but isn't remembered by any of the relevant parties, and the body which experienced it can be summed up as follows: a dress that is hung from a balustrade is not the container of your decay but decay's tissue wrapping.

LUMINOUS

No woman, specifically.

CHILD

We laugh and rejoice, drinking fair rejoinders beneath it.

LUMINOUS

She, specificity of "she," or …

HERONE

The flesh-toned dress, or spring.

CHILD

Death's sequined system of relatability.

Enter MATERNAL LOVE.

MATERNAL LOVE

You're already partaking in the performance, though you do not yet know it.

LUMINOUS

If she ...

Exit CHILD and MATERNAL LOVE.

HEROINE turns and addresses the audience.

HEROINE

The stage is a forthcoming garden, relating its sustenance in a litmus of spontaneity. How much longer will things remain the same? I haven't been able to rid myself of this countenance whose locale sources its sustaining in impossibility. I haven't been able to purge myself of this blessing (though its sadness repeals).

I don't deserve it. Every impossibility is, in essence, a former sensation.

LUMINOUS

(*under suggestion*) *Of she, framed.*

Enter MATERNAL LOVE.

MATERNAL LOVE

Sometimes the experience of will and affectation is a retreat whose landscape is chronology.

HEROINE

Sadness exists as a form of bargaining which may, at times, come to rest upon perfection.

(*singing laboriously*)

This anguished edge, this sole living perfection.
Is it mine?

MATERNAL LOVE

The chronology of this landscape is a stone causeway and the rising of day.

Enter CHILD. Exit MATERNAL LOVE.

LUMINOUS

Framing, she'd be in her infamy.

CHILD

This bird having now flowered within my distaste.

LUMINOUS

Flex, she'd be coated in lament.

HEROINE

I tore the copy and brought it inwards to reside in you, then retracing my image through a labour of future hesitancy and indecision.

The fallen snow was undeserved ...

(*singing*)

Still, it fell.
Still, it fell.
I beheld it in my sadness.

CHILD

Irretrievable judgment!

THIS SAD SCATTERING OF SIGNS

What authenticity does the light portend? I merge intuitively through adored rooms, singularly diurnal. Where interior is not readily distinguishable, so light slips readily into accusation.

CHORUS

Is the emptiness of the
image always aligned?

Is the force of the rain's
reckoning and distaste

As it falls,
a pre-emptive subjectivity?

This selfsame encounter

establishing exterior
With an excision of chance

and the falling
of this rain (as it falls

,

Always the
rain as it falls

ANTI-CHORUS

The
reckoning and

then

Encounter establishing
exterior

of this rain (as it falls
,

rain as it falls. ♪

ANTI-CHORUS

force of the rain's
distaste,

♪ as it falls,
falling.

with an
excision of chance,

♪ and the falling

♪ always

TO PERCEIVE INSTABILITY IN TERMS OF A FORMULAIC TOWER

Upon this fictive balcony I become able to perceive your equally fictive unbecoming.

HEROINE
This unearthed beauty – a field.

LUMINOUS
A decanter housed in instability.

CHILD
This beauty is a field. You must know it …

Enter MATERNAL LOVE.

MATERNAL LOVE
This field lined in marigold, you must know it …

LUMINOUS
A broad form of brevity.

Exit MATERNAL LOVE.

HEROINE
That the beauty of this field be recomposed beyond the severity of marigolds falling in among themselves, giving way to blossom at the edge of desire: this image composes the field's intractable boundary.

CHILD
This beauty must be filled.

LUMINOUS
In a waveform of brevity.

CHILD
The beauty of this field has been retracted.

LUMINOUS
A decanter housed in instability.

HEROINE
Don't try to establish me in the midst of my indifference.

CHILD
The beauty of this field has been retracted.

POINTS TOWARDS DIFFERENTIATION

Beauty's sharpened intellect raises a platform over which words pose exterior. Someone has awakened, hand in hand with similitude. The fever was only a document within the dream, yet its flushed prescription persists.

There is a singular light whose relevance relates to the darkness persisting alongside: only certain creatures wish to live by the incomplete light cast by stars.

resemblance.

CHORUS

How I imagine
the delirium of your face
might appear,

♪ In those days,
the hand?
♪ In those days,
♪ In those days,
encounter?
♪ In those days,
impression of
a dull ache in
♪ In those days,
together?

ANTI-CHORUS

♪ Might you
♪ Might you

Written,
drawn,
outlined:

The
bluish vigour of
resemblance.

It is
how I imagine
the
delirium of
your face
might
appear after
awakening.

In those days,
did you lead me by the
hand?

In those days,
did you?

In those days,
were you a believing
transparency?

Written,
drawn,
outlined:

afterwards.

did you lead me by

did you?
were you a believing

did the teething
loss already manifest
the seamless present?
did we simply sit

have ever loved me?
have? ♪

LATENESS (A PLATED BAUBLE)

A new atmosphere precedes change.

To glance reciprocally against fear is to vanish beneath a bodily insistence (cruel fever, battling rudiments of portrayal), is to allow a forceful method to resume (feverish, you might manifest a sparse corner within).

HEROINE
Always, it will be summer.

CHILD
Always, the body gives as it needs, and only an aroma of salt may discern the warmth it raises from memory.

HEROINE
After a period of time involving ourselves with an intricate belief in distance, judgments were made among systems of vitality –

CHILD
We are leaving all stones to require an unturned exterior.

HEROINE
Distance permits this, citing the inevitability of innocence.

LUMINOUS
All as distance permits.

HEROINE
I sign it, indelibly. Still all matter has as its corresponding requisite a limit.

CHILD
Had we doubly envisaged this encounter (an equality furthered by despair)?

HEROINE
I fluctuate tangentially across the same means of resemblance.

LUMINOUS
The dawn transmits its intrusion.

CHILD
Still all matter deviates, striates –

HERONE

(*interrupting*) Divides, recombines in measure of its eventual disarray.

CHILD

(*solemnly*) Finitude is finally dispersing.

LUMINOUS

(*folds upon an occasion of remorse*)

HEROINE

Where the breakage of an interior can, at times, reach into the present, causing it to peel, revealing an edge by which you may tear the entire thing away. So in my mourning, I might become capable of seeing what it is you are able to see, then inheriting myself through the specificity of your despair.

LUMINOUS

(*retraces her love*)

CHILD

Is putting words to an experience also one of a mask's many iterations?

LUMINOUS

To systematically attempt to ingest –

HEROINE

I thought I loved the dream.

CHILD

The heroine encounters doubt. She does not falter, but casts light upon it. A bent shadow appears.

LUMINOUS

Language in this case will, by necessity …

HEROINE

I loved, solely.

CHILD

Living as I did, living as I had come to accept …

LUMINOUS

(*pause*) *Come to fail upon resemblance.*

Enter MATERNAL LOVE.

MATERNAL LOVE

This detachment of figure preceding certain spatial recognitions: the corresponding brick wall differed in consistency from the wall adjacent to the window, again causing certain inconsistencies to become apparent.

Exit MATERNAL LOVE.

LUMINOUS

In ultimate preponderance.

CHILD

Speaking beneath the surface of articulation: a speaking accented with growth. Your bright and searing belief, sieve-like.

HEROINE

I was in love, solely.

BROAD DUNES (SPARED DOWNPOUR)

If it's raining, we have broadened this boundary with survival.

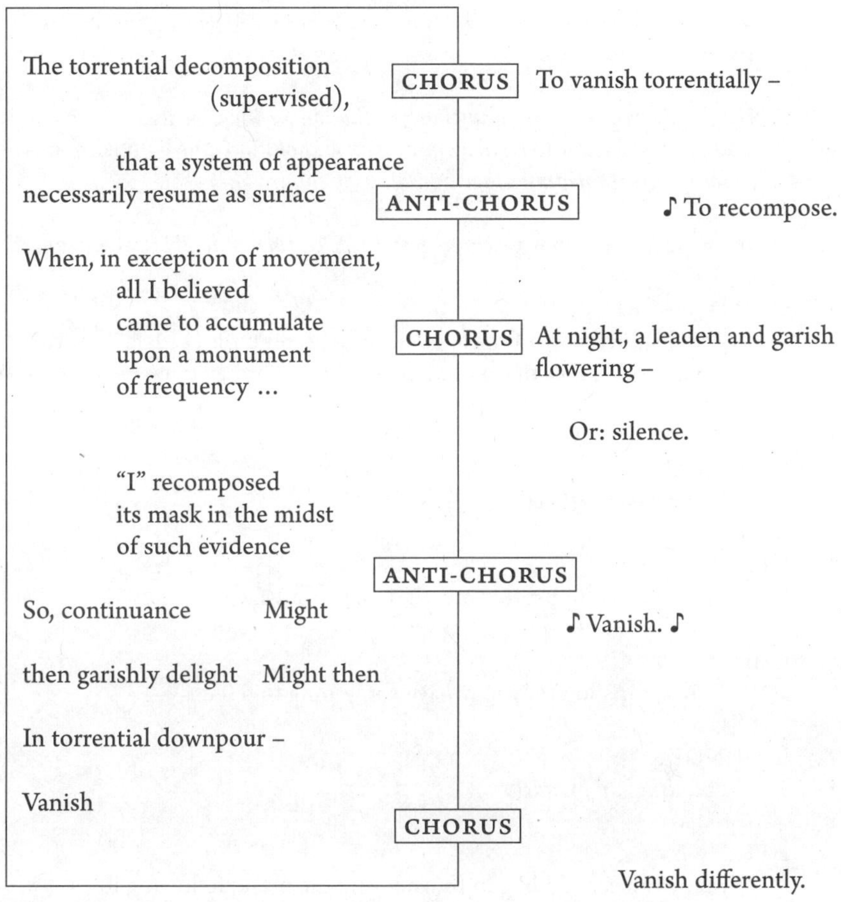

The torrential decomposition
(supervised),
CHORUS
To vanish torrentially –
that a system of appearance
necessarily resume as surface
ANTI-CHORUS
♪ To recompose.
When, in exception of movement,
all I believed
came to accumulate
upon a monument
of frequency …
CHORUS
At night, a leaden and garish
flowering –
Or: silence.
"I" recomposed
its mask in the midst
of such evidence
ANTI-CHORUS
So, continuance
Might
♪ Vanish. ♪
then garishly delight
Might then
In torrential downpour –
Vanish
CHORUS
Vanish differently.

FORESHADOWING A GARDEN

The limit to the reality presented becomes treacherous, enclosed. A formulaic interchange of light and shadow trigger a tactile need to exit the space, to cease witness. A passageway is created: a door. What we expect our gaze to refract has already been diverted.

The fragile frequency of an unchanged shadow or the degeneration of a certain kind of mask meant to exude what exists without intent is both itself and its opposite: the immediate stage and all it attempts to conceal.

The stage is uninhabited, echoic. Enter HEROINE and CHILD, estranged.

CHILD
The deathlessness of these floral ruins recombine a satisfactory ruse.
Come, let's dance upon our labours, for soon they must be harvested!

Enter LUMINOUS.

LUMINOUS
(*permits an artifact*)

HEROINE
I had wanted to protect myself, to cover my face.

CHILD
Dance, for soon they may have something to tell us!

LUMINOUS
(*punishes an artifact*)

HEROINE
Many times had I begun transmuting the mask, following its injury to its site of concealment, before realizing the path I'd inadvertently forged had led something else to me.

I thought that to dream repeatedly of the illuminated exterior was to cast difference into the irretrievable realm of substance, as though a too-clear representation of the unknown signalled its forthcoming implosion.

LUMINOUS
(*raises an artifact*)

CHILD
Dance soon! Dance soon!

HERONE

I am dancing! I am dancing!

LUMINOUS

(*renews an artifact*)

CHILD

I thought I could change the dream, but the dream changed me.

(*singing tonelessly to the rhythm of HEROINE's footsteps*) As a series would affirm any potentiality cast by motion mistaken for figure, as any potential overshadowed by theory or practice might suggest, we relate materiality to substance through veiled manners of suggestion by virtue of exterior, of past resemblance.

HEROINE ceases dancing.

HEROINE

As any series might affirm the cast-aside sequence of potential, so too might I adorn a flesh-toned exterior with sequins and silk, artifacts and lace.

LUMINOUS

(*splits an artifact*)

CHILD

On the balcony, over the fir tree, alongside a reminiscence vocalizing a back alley, on the balcony, over the fir tree, the balcony –

HEROINE

(*cutting off CHILD*) As any broken figure mistaken for mist, as any distant treasure mistaken for home, any disfigured intention released: I love you, I do.

LUMINOUS

(*portrays an artifact*)

HEROINE and CHILD resume dancing, clasped in a close embrace.

Enter MATERNAL LOVE.

MATERNAL LOVE

(*sobbing*) And theatres formed by the trees so full of potential.

Exit MATERNAL LOVE.

LUMINOUS

(*ingests an artifact*)

A PERCEPTIBLE FACE

In the pallor of a fissure.

	CHORUS	
I overheard myself	The effect	in my world,
bandaged in	Of this watching, knows	unredeemed grasping of
exterior.	perception is contingent	
It rained upon this	The effect	world,
rained upon the	Which of its watching	ulterior of substance –
It rained upon	is contingent, paperless	eternity's vague material.
	abstraction	
It rained upon		motive, it rained upon fault.
	Whose effect is	
	knowing	
	Likewise watching	
While everything,	Effect:	insensate and drained
and dripping from	Hesitancy	trees still recovering from
	reducing errancy	downpour –
	to suggestion	
Mostly that the sky		was so pale, inevitable.
And the dawn		which had appeared so sharply
		differentiated,
when it finally did		appear –

VISIBLE AT A DISTANCE

A generally occurring loss might betray tenderness towards that which has been lost but remains incapable of any means of reconstruction: that of possession (likeliness which may be reconstructed through dialogue), that of memory (truly of and within itself), that of appearance (which is physically resumed). The manner by which the apparent remains unalike fluctuates, each uncanny divergence rehabilitating and restructuring sanctity in the midst of its transformation.

CHILD and LUMINOUS are not present on the stage.

Enter HEROINE.

HEROINE

(*covering her face with an expressionless mask of paper*) Why do you look at me this way. Why must you treat me in this manner. Is it something I did. Why did you tie it so tight. You tied it too tight – look, it's dead. Look, you killed it. Why do you act as though loss is always forthcoming, yet when it arrives, it has already relocated behind you. Had you not seen it. Had you welcomed it into your home. It could not have entered unless you had allowed it to enter.

Enter MATERNAL LOVE.

MATERNAL LOVE

(*whispering*) This is a good way to control the circulation of strangers within your space.

Exit MATERNAL LOVE.

HEROINE

Did you ever love me. Had you ever. Tell me now. Tell me, for I must know how far away I need to be from you in order to begin again. Someone told someone else that they felt as though they had fallen from the back of a moving vehicle. Someone told someone else that no matter where they went they felt this terrible, inexpressible rage having no object. Someone told someone else that it was their fault. Someone told someone else that something happened they did not remember until that moment. That is not quite what I feel, perhaps something similar. Have you ever fallen a great distance and only remembered many years later. Have you. Have you. How do you know what that would feel like. How could you. How could you possibly know. How could you possibly know what that would feel like.

HEROINE removes her mask, revealing a flickering countenance.

Enter MATERNAL LOVE.

MATERNAL LOVE

How long did this sensation stay with you after the event? For how long has this sensation persisted? Why are you so certain that what you are feeling is this sensation in particular?

Exit MATERNAL LOVE.

HEROINE puts the mask back on, again concealing her face.

HEROINE

Why is this diffuse, circulatory meaning already so damaged. Why have I laid this carpet. Memory is a portrayal of innocence, always. At least for me, this is the case. I say this without intent to induce envy or lust. Innocence, though somehow the present conceals it. Only later feeling the full extent of my weakness, my powerlessness to carry time. My inability to carry time is a sensation with no source. At times I sense my skin interacting with something that isn't there. Then the carpet is rolled and stored away for summer. Moments in any season of feeling its loss. Or the already occurring loss of which we are peripherally aware. I already know there is no carpet. In between mimicry and abandon, something I have planted. In between abandon and spite, something I have planted reaching past the space I have allowed it, the space I had emptied for it; intersecting with the space I have allowed myself, the space I had emptied for myself.

Uncontrolled growth exists in between sadness and rage. There exists no carpet. No carpet, but allow me to sleep briefly upon its weft before waking.

II

SHE DREAMS A GRIEVOUS OMISSION

LUMINOUS

(*asleep*) A field, circumstantially believed
Reveals its intransience in stages

A route may be established
A route through a field

May then be determined
Love maintains it

As does the equivalence of this
Or any other capacity maintain itself in me

Today, I am wearing my disappearance
A perennial veil

Appearance beginning by day
Forthright veils of sapphire or obedience

Forthright veils of roses
And their concurrent foundations

I'm working on a humid, unwritten newness
Whose persistence bodies daybreak

Crossing over from a witnessing sleep (terror)
Into matter's winded remorse (counter-terror)

I escaped into a sleeping emanation (terror)
Into a muscular allowance of forms (counter-terror)

You have my confidence, you codified wind
You rageless thaw, even you (even you)

Must know enough to bow
Beneath the litmus of a whisper

This street has amounted to nothing
But absence concurrent to a garden

The breeze, in crossing a threshold
Complicates skin with sensation

A garden is snowing
Scenically, a dune

In its failed defence, beauty
Has always been an act of irrelevance

I expected time to serve my indifference
And be afraid

I upended a scarred fruit, imprinted
Upon its own destitute survival

I expired, timorously, into a dim surge
Of dust, flawed with indivisible serenities

I performed fate
I performed fate

Believing I had hollowed a space
Of perfection and acuity

A crumbling column of fate held me in its mouth
It, too, was performative

It lived, and it was itself in me
That lived anew

It became a world
Dreaming upon cities of the dream

Dreaming upon the world
Dreaming upon the dream

I wanted time to sever my indifference
And be afraid

All I did not know – the endlessness of day
All I was unable to express in full awareness

Now bereft, disclosed
All I defeated in residence to waiting

A remorseful image which might have been myself
(Or myself seen from a distance)

Image disclosing the meaning
Of delay to both myself

And those anticipated
Whose regressive approach followed defeatedly after absence

Transforming into something
Even more distant and useless to me

Are the figures within the image
Only impartially lit?

The background silhouette of rain
A shorthand indicating event?

The breeze which casts its sensation is an illuminating field
While the illegibility of locale begets a city of precedents

I mentor my indifference with distinction
Won't this requiring subjectivity

Also fail
Underhandedly?

Won't this beauty become bearable?
While the rain's legibility also falls

I can't feel anything
I can't feel time passing me by

The feeling of this transit
Bearing towards the sun

Or a thought of the cold
"How rich I am," I told myself

Beyond its collusive angle of defence
The rain has not damaged this figural garden

Whose space begets an intimacy of appearing
I have so evidently failed it, I have damaged it anew!

Due to the possibility of dusk
Being tied to me, I again became capable

Of imagining the relevance of a changed visage
Wherein potential's charge gave way to acuity

Gave way to an embalmed beauty, gave way
In a representational manner –

The road came to body
A structural gloss

That which bodied its distinction in subject
Then called itself to me –

As with any sadness witnessed
Among the sunless gardens of others

All must turn its perceiving face
Towards the light

The rain has not damaged this figural garden
Whose space begets an intimacy of appearing

This humanness is yours to hold
(It must suffice)

Evidently, I have failed it
(Failed it anew)

In defiant rejection of the road
I passed along a noisome river

Sharpened with the distinct filigree of wings
And the adjacent call of birds

Distractedly recommending themselves
Across the paired sensitivity of the world

You must believe this system of possibility
Receives its subject

As does this subject receive itself
As a semblance of that undifferentiated world?

I can still see every ended image
The finitude of what appears in relief

Irreproachably alike
Sky pacing the trace of a path

And I, what of it?
What of the self which exists

To equal or greater exclusion within
To this rain which has not damaged us

And yet exceedingly, falls
What of the world which exists beside it?

What of this exceeding thinness
Concurrent to being awake

Any number of dreams preceding iteration
Whose recognition repeals

Adjacency's fragant intimacy?
I tore the veil from my skin

Yet a dense residue remained
This rainfall goes far beyond itself

What changed city has this become?
Unavoidably, I no longer seek it in me

You might know of this vanished route
And I, who haven't yet traversed it

These expressive occlusions
Creases dampened in futility's unseeing warp

What shall serve as a guide to the changed city?
Any unsanctified passage will do

Failing that, a veil
Figural blossoms related with cruelty

Akin to vista and visage
A rose

Torn from appearing
A rose, indefinitely raised to variousness

(A rose)
I would rather pass by such defeat

Than propose limit to encounter
I would rather pass by (meekly)

The content of this evasion is euphoric
Constitutive of a grieving passage

Whose defeated momentum
May then be cast asunder

Cast away into the means a city has
Cast away into the alleys or conduits or shelves of a city

Cast into the revolving doors, the hanging walls
The façades of a city

A refracted surface bearing inevitability
A city, relating in essence what it had dreamed –

Which I had dreamed
From any number of dreams

To speak of it …
To speak of it …

I suppose I've codified resemblance
For such misfortunes are indicative of a passageway

Or of disastrous fates
I don't even desire it

This ruling cast beneath ground
Perseverance reaching beyond itself

Beyond perpetuity
So does the day preclude involuntary flourishing

As does the night constrict events of day
Retreating into a shadowy figure of itself

Stop saying you recognize my suffering
And I, what of it?

I escaped into a sleeping immanence
Limit contextualizing its diversion

Diversion indicating its attention
Through nettled cupolas, cupolas

Of supplication, derivative cupolas, fantastical –
Have I caused you harm?

I would rather divide ceaselessly into your gaze
I would rather betray origin than betray ...

Have I caused you harm?
I would rather assuage this graceless category ...

Did rain degrade us in the city?
I would rather ...

Through a brief assemblage of disbelief
I encountered it peaceably

I harmed, vanished
Within the guilt of my supposition

I cast myself away
That which you find yourself able to believe

What can you believe
That has not already been taken from me?

I ask only to indicate my inability
To delimit your love for finite things

Of which I am one (most certainly)
From adorative excesses

Whose weight is only seasoned (limited by)
Irreproachable beauty (i.e., of this night

This Mesozoic lake, this unloved
Becoming, this bodied

Asymmetrically) – from this precedent
Now context to your disloyalty

Whose instability stems
From my rigid belief in beauty

There's a clue stuck in the fissures of my becoming
Of course wings will fall silent as they pass over

This is the general fulfillment of all that is certain
My great belief is that I will also persist

Dreaming into this convulsing node
Of disappearance

You're running around an irreproachable wound
(Of course you are)

I closed the door
I closed the code

Closed myself to the spring
Essentially, I was fatally decisive

For rain unearths us where we are
In fruitless recovery does it face us with indifference

I had hollowed myself out to fate
Leaving a small space in which I might receive

Some journey of shock or retrieval
My indifference as it vanished

Bent by an arbitrary sleight of hand –
Vast, irreproachable absurdities

To speak of this ...
In imitation, loving and being loved

To speak of the vague sounding
Of daylight I have now disallowed

Or the dream's violence
Where once again, snow covered

Everything
I found it at my feet

When I awoke
I wore it through the rain

It shielded my face
From the sun …

I fear luminance is becoming upset with me
Finitude must have its rules

I had myself
To likewise illuminate both rule and its clause

The exception:
Destiny

Passing at a rate too slow to perceive
Yet to come

Destiny …
Destiny …

A fluttering out of the corner of mine eye
See how the light fades it

How tenderly light
Casts deficiency into the dream

Destiny …
Destiny …

This still light will suffice (solely)
With such ease, this still-sufficient sun

This still sun
Will suffice

As it must suffice
As we must wake within

That which we must not awaken.

LUMINOUS awakens.

III

THIS SURPASSING WHICH RECALLS THE WORLD

❋ AND AGAIN, A ROSE ❋ A FIGURATIVE GLANCE ❋ A FICTIVE RESPONSE ❋ THE WORLD'S PRICELESS WRECKAGE, WORDLESS INTERIORITIES OF RESONANCE AND REPLICATION – GARDENS OF ROSES – GARDENS OF INTUITION – GARDENS AND GARDENS AND GARDENS ❋ ALCHEMIC BONDS ❋ THE ADDITIONAL SEASON: CIRCULATORY FIXATION OR, LOCALE, THE FIXITY OF A BREEZE ❋ EFFORTLESS AFFRONT ❋ THE WORD FOR A KIND OF FUGITIVITY PERMITTING A CONDITION OF SUSTENANCE ❋ GERMINATING ❋ A GARDEN BOUND TO A STORM ❋ A ROSE HAS OVEREXTENDED INTO A SEMBLANCE OF PURE APPEARANCE

AND AGAIN, A ROSE

To unveil contextual heights in all their anguish, yes, to snow in recombination.
To inherit the seeming of any exterior, to counter. Yes, to snow in recombination.
Repealing illusive contours of exchange, yes, to snow in affective recombination.

ANTI-CHORUS (*prophetically*)

That the room
already exists ...

♪

CHORUS

I manage
I manage

Deeply willed
accumulation,
I withheld

ANTI-CHORUS

Because
mine, I released

Formulaically,
amplification renews an
occurrent line of will

Formulaically,
a gaze begets its own renewal

If amplification occurs, so does
that abject room

(doubly
appearing

That uncollected field
(whose grasses resume
an unburdened line

That willed body of water
(crystalline

That dissimilar fold
(

That abject

room)

of your abjection

(somewhere).

a discursive division,
as well as I am able.

within body's

an uncollected field.

the language was
it.

CHORUS

A FIGURATIVE GLANCE

Try to willfully induce the obscurity of a mask of beauty, its ever-persistent removal from rote manifestations of daily existence; the sense of trepidation it tends to induce/redact/inscribe. The mask is ever contained within the shielded present. This is the essence of its horror – the true unremarkability of that which has been attenuated to appear beautiful but whose beauty is not only an illusion, but a vacancy gazing into reversion. All this has already been established; in essence, the beautiful mask is true horror.

What then, does this reversion appear as?

HEROINE
I perceived the edge as a limitless exterior, garnished with ribbon, both its extraneousness and fragility in this way highlighted.

LUMINOUS
In satin circulation, unimpeded.

HEROINE
I watch you blending immersive entities over the shores of repression.

CHILD
This distance now concealed by clouds.

LUMINOUS
Silencing upon contact with skin.

HEROINE
In complete absorption, you circulate through means of a questioning known to you alone. In complete abstraction you circulate within the breeze, among trees, filing satin indifference into articulation (an imprint so often mistaken for the sound of something falling from a wall or table).

LUMINOUS
Becoming matted with subverted lust and hair.

HEROINE
Many times, had I suspected my mask was beginning to reveal something I hadn't nurtured, something not of my own but anterior to having, to possession, wilful or otherwise ...

CHILD

Many times, had I inspected the mask in darkness after you had fallen asleep, questioning the depths of the spaces left for my face to sense, questioning the silence and validity of its uninhabited composure.

HEROINE

There is someone at the door.

Enter MATERNAL LOVE.

MATERNAL LOVE

So a scalpel might become a seam ripper, a needle, an unshielded razor, a breeze alternating through fixity.

HEROINE

Who will answer the door?

Exit MATERNAL LOVE.

CHILD

So a scalpel might become lover or child or body or surface, coexisting in the space of separation.

HEROINE

The door ... will you answer it?

A FICTIVE RESPONSE

I imagine you in a garden of roses, sprayed differently in colour, its rarity and beauty causing the transformation of garden into cupola.

I hung sheer curtains of antique lace over the windows. I bought you a new dress. It is all as it ought to be, as both lace and roses are unassailable evidence that there is daylight.

Lace and dresses, incontrovertible as dreams.

ANTI-CHORUS (*emotive*)

Repeat, Repeal,
Return, Repeal,
Resume,
Recede,
Repeat, Repeat,
Renew,
Repeat, Repeal,
Return, Repeal,
Resume,
Recede,
Repeat, Repeat,
Renew,
Repeat, Repeal,
Return, Repeal,
Resume,
Recede,
Repeat, Repeat,
Renew,
Repeat, Repeal,
Return, Repeal,
Resume,
Recede,
Repeat, Repeat,
Renew,
Repeat,
Repeal,
Return, Repeal,
Resume,
Recede,
Repeat,
Repeat, Renew,

The detached form of a fixture: ♪ Repeat.

The detached form of a fixture: ♪ Repeal.

♪ The woman enters the room.
♪ The woman renews the contract.
♪ The woman redacts the crime.

Entirely subsumed by connective tissue, a fixture:
♪ Return.

When the fixture undressed to reveal the fine texture of pinprick beading:
♪ Repeal.

When the fixture, redressed, disclosed only a shutter of opaque silk:
♪ Resume.

♪ The woman's crime is suspect.
♪ The woman, too, is suspect.
♪ Suspect is the crime committed.
♪ Suspect is the perpetrator of the crime.
♪ Suspect, too, is the placeholder from which crime occurs.
♪ Suspect, too, is the figure enclosed within.
♪ Suspect is the one who carries it.

To be propelled across a hallway, levitant, scarcely setting foot upon it: ♪ Recede.

Prior to a secondary level, perhaps beneath ground, a closet: ♪ Repeat.
Prior to a secondary level, perhaps beneath ground, a closet: ♪ Repeat.
Prior to a secondary level, perhaps beneath ground, a closet: ♪ Renew.

♪ The woman redacts the crime.
♪ The woman renews the contract.
♪ The woman leaves the room. ♪

THE WORLD'S PRICELESS WRECKAGE, WORDLESS INTERIORITIES OF RESONANCE AND REPLICATION – GARDENS OF ROSES – GARDENS OF INTUITION – GARDENS AND GARDENS AND GARDENS

A torn rose (worn in lieu of a shield).
A torn rose worn as a dress (worn in lieu of a shield).
A dress is worn (worn in lieu of a shield).

The roses remain beautiful in excess, though indiscreetly dyed.
The floral disclosure of nearness conveying an irretrievable tension: every surface is retinal.

Rain is falling. All at this moment, no longer.

LUMINOUS
In downpour.

HEROINE
I misplaced a mistaken assemblage.

CHILD
A vanillic, procedural garden.

HEROINE
A luminous grove.

LUMINOUS
(*constructs an artifact*)

HEROINE
I couldn't otherwise, with such vehemence, adore this cold, silver curfew, composure posturing itself in tedium, cleaving the substance of its sustaining with wrath.

LUMINOUS
(*poses a question*)

HEROINE
What formality do I expect from the universe?

CHILD
For the sun to manoeuvre between leaves?

Enter MATERNAL LOVE.

MATERNAL LOVE

Where else can I keep you? Within the wind's wrecked sentencing?

Exit MATERNAL LOVE.

HEROINE

I've reduced your waiting to a faded exteriority (in this way I always have).

LUMINOUS

Law circumvents us ...

CHILD

Dawn passes through finite drapery, tortuously laced. How beautiful ...

LUMINOUS

... as with a transiting breeze ...

HEROINE

(*ignoring CHILD*) A dress worn in lieu of a shield betrays ... betrays itself!

LUMINOUS

... betrays the brushed legibility of its discolouration ...

CHILD

(*startled*) The dress is too large ... it has fallen from my shoulders!

HEROINE

(*ignoring CHILD*) I've reduced your waiting to a fold.

LUMINOUS

... to indelible artifact.

CHILD

The dress, it has fallen ...

HEROINE

(*ignoring CHILD*) Is it raining outside? Is it?

CHILD

Is the hesitation occurring before the falling of the rain essential to it or to me? The dress has been ruined ...

HERONE

(*ignoring CHILD*) In complete abstraction, I fail you.

CHILD

In the enormity of my abstraction, I have failed.

Exit CHILD. Enter MATERNAL LOVE.

MATERNAL LOVE

The heroine will say …

HEROINE and MATERNAL LOVE

(*together*) I want to damage you; I always have.

Exit MATERNAL LOVE.

ALCHEMIC BONDS

A star handled with ease, whose bared touch shears porosity. Thus, a star (gloved). A star whose uninhabited touch shears containment, wherein touch transmits itself referentially. Wherein whatever touch permits induces a contract though which surface comes to be employed.

ANTI-CHORUS

Why
might sever
persistence.
Why
the source.

That which turns away from itself
Fails from a subtracted luminescence
of effects
Whose remains turn away
from the contracted stage
of renewal

Your defacement
is a relative transversal.
a glass panel of remittance
afterthought at its root of

CHORUS
ANTI-CHORUS
CHORUS
ANTI-CHORUS

The road turns away from itself
The road returns from a
beheld effacement
The road beholds its dereliction
The road turns away from itself

I'm not different.

♪ Why not?

I
missing and
it is,

To disabuse yourself
Of the circularity of effect
This grasping
In the midst of sustenance
Your defacement:

know what is both
immanent,
in a sense, obvious.

"What is bravery, its compulsions
and true destination?"

"I haven't a clue.
Possibility is so
irrelevant to me."

THE ADDITIONAL SEASON: CIRCULATORY FIXATION or, LOCALE, THE FIXITY OF A BREEZE

With danger and lenience, a breeze circulates through prior conduits of form (a patio chair, the haricots verts, *the untied trellis, the disassembled brick). Form's fixity (an early brushing of water, a sore imprint marked upon pliability, a terracotta basin containing unseeded loam) is a hollow interior which needs to be aired (seasonally). The breeze recreates (as in recreation, as in sojourn, as in harmonious unattachment) or aerates (as in questions poetically, Socratically, or mathematically) under this particular locus of resemblance, producing mimetic atmospheres (conditions) for change: difference may manifest depending on a general mood, mobility, motivity – an occasion might inherit rain, then, or disgust; aridity.*

The breeze only counters resemblance by moving it to tastefully occupy a more vigorous locale.

CHILD

This tedious transit through unbodied form ...

LUMINOUS

Such curtains change.

CHILD

The colour through which an aspect comes to be illuminated ...

LUMINOUS

A face, startlingly beginning to differ.

Enter MATERNAL LOVE.

MATERNAL LOVE

Slanting, a scalpel might end its belligerence by finally being put to unexpected use.

Exit MATERNAL LOVE.

HEROINE

I am dying (hesitantly) between hydrated pathways.

CHILD

So might a scalpel become interspersed with silk.

Enter MATERNAL LOVE.

MATERNAL LOVE

The heroine must, of course, perish prematurely, by her own means. This being a righteous and justifiable end.

Exit MATERNAL LOVE.

HEROINE

As further habits of predestination force validity to recombine into fissure, recollection, or solidity –

MATERNAL LOVE

To involve a seeming expression of ease within the lacquer signals great craftsmanship. To allow the face to come to speak is a mythic feat, perhaps existing only in lore.

HEROINE

In lore ... meant for children?

Exit MATERNAL LOVE.

CHILD

A dream that you killed all of the flies at once, I, covering their bodies in salt to ensure they would not wake.

HEROINE

That which falters is only taking a moment to rehearse and recompose to its most advantageous visage.

LUMINOUS

The muscle willing itself to release instead contracts.

CHILD

For your seriousness: a casing.

HEROINE

For your collision: a code.

LUMINOUS

Who smiled?

Enter MATERNAL LOVE.

MATERNAL LOVE

Say nothing. There is no need for you to speak.

Exit MATERNAL LOVE.

LUMINOUS

Waking, aflame ...

CHILD

Wearied, I positioned alterity in relation to our composure.

LUMINOUS

... passed through figure, into your arms.

HEROINE

Reticent, I assumed.

LUMINOUS

Your arms then receiving me without ambiguity, without expectation.

CHILD and HEROINE

(*unseen*) I aligned, with precision, uncontested measures of chance.

EFFORTLESS AFFRONT

The starless weight of gain is a spiteful equanimity. As probability might cast its redirection in a manner supposing your relevance, so must fate necessitate more than an alteration of that which has already passed. An unforetold changing of the immutable, the pastoral, the already imbibed, the mnemonic, the dreamed, occurs beyond each simultaneity.

There can be no messenger.

ANTI-CHORUS

<table>
<tr><td>Flower,</td><td></td><td>gratitude!</td></tr>
<tr><td>This</td><td></td><td>morning is</td></tr>
<tr><td>what has brought</td><td></td><td>you here,</td></tr>
<tr><td>to me!</td><td></td><td></td></tr>
<tr><td></td><td>That unbirthed quality by which you appear –</td><td></td></tr>
<tr><td>Stroking the</td><td>Mention it! With acuity,</td><td>bleeding,</td></tr>
<tr><td>irritative torso</td><td>it appears With gratitude</td><td></td></tr>
<tr><td>♪</td><td></td><td>of clarity,</td></tr>
<tr><td>I came to</td><td>The quality</td><td>believe</td></tr>
<tr><td>♪</td><td>of your appearing</td><td>in</td></tr>
<tr><td>affliction.</td><td>In assemblage, negates</td><td></td></tr>
<tr><td></td><td>true appearance.</td><td></td></tr>
<tr><td></td><td></td><td>Finally, in</td></tr>
<tr><td></td><td>Of gratitude, nothing.</td><td>mind,</td></tr>
<tr><td>I saw it</td><td></td><td>with</td></tr>
<tr><td>solidity:</td><td>I speak only of Roses</td><td></td></tr>
<tr><td>the</td><td>Catering the edges between transformation</td><td>distinction</td></tr>
<tr><td>you had mentored.</td><td></td><td></td></tr>
<tr><td></td><td>Roses by which have also occurred by another</td><td></td></tr>
<tr><td>Clarity</td><td>name</td><td>unspooling</td></tr>
<tr><td>long allergic</td><td>By whose unmoved quality also appears –</td><td>symbols</td></tr>
<tr><td>distinct</td><td></td><td>within</td></tr>
<tr><td>sensory bodies.</td><td>Unmentionable surface</td><td></td></tr>
<tr><td>♪</td><td>(Unmentioned)</td><td>The sun,</td></tr>
<tr><td>simply – ♪</td><td></td><td></td></tr>
<tr><td></td><td></td><td>Simply.</td></tr>
</table>

THE WORD FOR A KIND OF FUGITIVITY PERMITTING A CONDITION OF SUSTENANCE

The stage was a caged petal posed at the core of an unbelieving, the means of its construction remaining impenetrable and gorgeous, leaking.

HEROINE

I had believed we were meant to perpetuate fate, to possess it as we gradually descended indistinct stairs into adoration or envy –

CHILD

Though the rain then fell through it.

HEROINE

Though the rain then fell through my conviction.

Enter MATERNAL LOVE.

MATERNAL LOVE

The first-hand subjectivity of an intention (intuitive) – whose requiring ossifies.

CHILD

The word's appreciative wreckages find no fault.

MATERNAL LOVE

Denial ossifies, where ossification is a precedent through and among any parallel arrangement of forms.

Exit MATERNAL LOVE.

HEROINE

Disgust maintains, as its solitary object, the only one capable of shouldering it: myself. I need it from you, too, my disgust – it needs you as much as it needs me. I don't hesitantly cast myself against this wall. There isn't hesitation; there's you and there's me.

CHILD

Against the dawn whose rising, willed concurrence is unnecessary.

HEROINE

Forced to turn to you, I still close my eyes, seeing what's there. Your debasement (is it mine?) is hidden from me foremost.

CHILD

Please don't continue in this defacement.

Enter MATERNAL LOVE.

MATERNAL LOVE

Why wait behind the blindness of time? This exceeding thinness of qualitative concern and fruitless indifference ...

There can be no origination for that which precipitates impossibility.

A cold lesson within the sigh of encounter: essence is a divergent excision. To me, this dispersal of event relative to my position is only a remnant.

Exit MATERNAL LOVE.

LUMINOUS

Is notation.

HEROINE

Continue.

GERMINATING

I am such as spring in recurrence relates its abhorrent position.
I am such as the decaying remnants of illusion invoke their relative excess.
I am such as the gold-plated abjection of exterior begins to address its shame (likewise gilded).

And yet potential persists as unreserved process. Persistence begets alteration.
And yet an unchanged referent gathers upon the persistent plane of survival like a storm.

CHORUS (*embodied*)

		A
storm,	Engage me on these terms	exceedingly
	... has turned to storm	ancient.
A storm,		outlined.
	Engage me on these terms	
A	... as turned into storm	storm,
closing		itself
	On the terms of the storm	to
	... I felt an affinity with the skies	intermittence.
	“And so the rain falls”	Moving
across the	“And so the wind was remade	boundary, I
am so loved,	into excision”	
I am	“And so cancellation repeals”	
my suffering.	“and so”	
	“and so”	
	“and so”	♪ Sound
		sweeping
		through a page.
		♪ Sound
		sweeping
		through a page.

A GARDEN BOUND TO A STORM

Futurity hinges on a glance concealed beneath winter. All that upholds itself as a force of renewal concedes this fiction – that of both suspicion and its remorse. As between a curtain and its shade, a momentary lapse where continuity pauses and will not enter.

A blown-out interiority spills transactionally into the visible.

As between a rose and a rose's perceptual decay, a moment of fullness hesitating indefinitely on the edge of turning.

CHILD is not present on the stage.

HEROINE

This terrible needlessness overshadows all. Watch carefully. Watch how the resinous material of transience collects in repetitious serenity over finitude's unlimited edges.

These rehearsals make their address to fate itself, whose tall yawns of discomfort obscure the dawn's increasing earliness.

LUMINOUS

(*fails an exterior*)

Enter MATERNAL LOVE.

MATERNAL LOVE

Alternatively, a territoriality.

HEROINE

How are we to manage this terrible materiality? Must we remain on loan to it forever, sentenced to a longing requiring only emptiness as its object? I wanted more than that for us.

LUMINOUS

(*fails upon a surface*)

MATERNAL LOVE

That decision was not yours to make.

LUMINOUS

Beneath.

HEROINE
Then whose?

MATERNAL LOVE
Not your own.

HEROINE
Then whose?

MATERNAL LOVE
My own ...

LUMINOUS
Beneath my belief.

HEROINE
Where might I now turn in order to establish the exceeding thinness of this façade? Such beautiful balustrades you have recovered, with such believable shadows.

The flowers, too, appear breathless.

HEROINE and MATERNAL LOVE begin waltzing between untrimmed rows of dandelions, sunflowers towering above.

HEROINE
These believable circuits have established several previously unforeseen certainties. Look – the street has been altered to renounce yet another name ...

It begins to rain. Droplets cast trembling shadows upon HEROINE and MATERNAL LOVE. The imprint of these shadows causes their faces to appear wet with tears, which causes HEROINE to begin sobbing uncontrollably.

MATERNAL LOVE
The flowers, too, appear breathless. Why, you are crying!

LUMINOUS
Beneath belief.

HEROINE
As are you.

A ROSE HAS OVEREXTENDED INTO A SEMBLANCE OF PURE APPEARANCE

A lived boundary of disbelief presents its material love. Appearance attracts a persuasive light. You pass into meltwater, betraying the season's first snow.

it fell where the rain willed it

CHORUS The rainfall

to fall, and with
great suggestive force
it
melted when snow's
time was done
it
drew me into it
as the soil, too,
required

goes beyond itself,

an instantaneous season
whose
correspondence

speech bodies
in suggestion.

♪ I

reduce its
implication.

this instantaneous
passage is a traversal
of intent and will

ANTI-CHORUS

A rose, on a pedestal,
might convince a shadow

of its offer.

I wrote to you across
a subjectless inquiry

A rose, solely,
might

then articulate
a song.

I wanted to demote
this veil of intuition:

I fell upon the rain

CHORUS

♪ This sadness
is my impossibility.

(as it then fell
upon me)

♪ This sadness is
my only sensation.

IV

SHE DREAMS UPON FIFTEEN STAGES

❋ BURN (STAGE 1) ❋ DEEPLY WITHHELD IMAGE, BOUND TO A STORM (STAGE 2) ❋ CERTITUDE IS THE SILVER OF WATER BETWEEN MOUNTAINS (STAGE 3) ❋ EACH DAY ENDING IN GRADATION AND SEVERITY (STAGE 4) ❋ EXPERIENTIALLY (STAGE 5) ❋ AND VANISHES (STAGE 6) ❋ OF LILIES (STAGE 7) ❋ AREAS OF EFFORTLESS AFFRONT UPON THE SAME ASHEN STAGE OF OCCURRENCE (STAGE 8) ❋ BLANK FILLIGREE GLOVES OF INTENT (STAGE 9) ❋ I MISREMEMBERED (STAGE 10) ❋ POTENTIAL CLARIFICATIONS (STAGE 11) ❋ THIS BEAUTY HAS BEEN CAST AFIELD (STAGE 12) ❋ AS NEWS OF THE SPECTACLE REACHED ME, I RETURNED MY FACE TO A SEMBLANCE OF DESIRE SO AS NOT TO BE EXPELLED FROM THE WHINING GARDEN (STAGE 13) ❋ IT IS NOT WITHIN MY TENDENCY TO MOVE NEGLIGENTLY THROUGH STORMS OF APPEARANCE (STAGE 14) ❋ A MOMENT BELIED (STAGE 15)

BURN (STAGE 1)

A silver field. The ambiguous, light-refracting quality of silver is regurgitated by the severity of a world's proximate distance.

LUMINOUS

I lost your name   deeply burnished –
threaded in vermeil, muscularly complete
an articulate field

– responsive

This is the futurity of my discourse
          [[[[you saw me
fade from the world   ] and as I
faded, you
faded too   We
faded
from the world with great acuity
          and unprecedented insight

It was our future.
You saw me there.

DEEPLY WITHHELD IMAGE, BOUND TO A STORM (STAGE 2)

The disastrous progression of logic displays its portraits upon a blank wall. The images expire as one passes. As of yet, one remains incapable of moving backwards in the passageway.

LUMINOUS

[in a deply withheld beauty]]]]
– rubbed raw [[[[burnished
beyond resistance] Fallen
between decisive agonies of loneliness,
retraction, separation –
Through repealed distances we became
unable to circumvent –
[[[[not even in dream!]

[not even in dream]]]]]
Wherein the same passage became replicated
[[[[to have thought it could be navigated
with the same freedom
and irreverence
(Falsity!)]

Even in the dream , unable
to become fully convinced
by a deeply withheld spontaneity –
The referencing of this occurrent dream

[[[[if this passage
arose] had arisen.

CERTITUDE IS THE SILVER OF WATER BETWEEN MOUNTAINS (STAGE 3)

A luminous hall of dolls and apology.

LUMINOUS

A glass margin has enveloped me
(with   gradation)
          in the gradual despondency of your
title, you had needed   to oppose me
with your silence]]]]] [[[your own unaware
 dullness a sensuality,   formulaic]

A faded star is an initial ambiguity

                    [Belated

          A faded star alters its surface with
          abundance –
                              [[[[[within the gradual
deteriorating light

                              coeval upon leaves]
I insisted, this is good earth, as it had been
                                        [I insisted

          the limpidity of this margin
          not be confused with transparency

          nor the limpidity of this margin
                    be refused.   ]

EACH DAY ENDING IN GRADATION AND SEVERITY (STAGE 4)

As though the shores established at the boundary of memory had been rinsed, disinfected – sands free of debris, replete. This perfection procedurally marred at the edges. Beyond which a matted logic of sea grass, shells, and cigarettes maintain. Systematic.

LUMINOUS

In the oceanic seeming of continuance,
I lost my name

[salient.

Beneath your name,
its tenor and sustaining mystery]]]

– each day within this garden
evolving]]

Each day in endless resolve
in vital lending in the given
formlessness of becoming

I searched …

In damaged fountains of creation, I found

[[I found there
]]

every lasting notion:

retrieval,
salience.

EXPERIENTIALLY (STAGE 5)

A greenhouse. Glass walls. A single white birdcage and a chair –

LUMINOUS

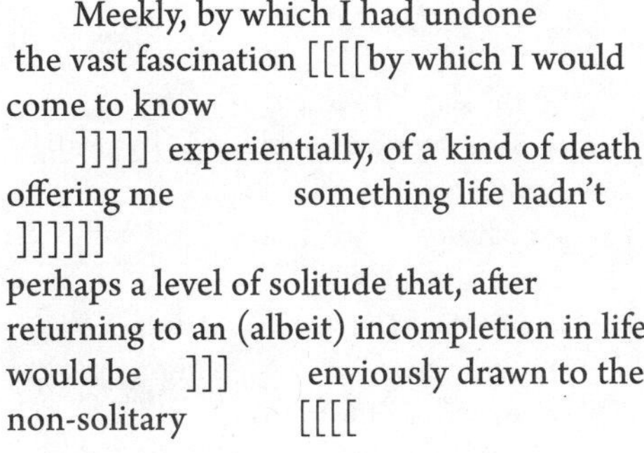

Meekly, by which I had undone
the vast fascination [[[[by which I would
come to know
]]]]] experientially, of a kind of death
offering me something life hadn't
]]]]]]
perhaps a level of solitude that, after
returning to an (albeit) incompletion in life
would be]]] enviously drawn to the
non-solitary [[[[

– that death might have something to
offer beyond this complete ownership, I
continued to doubt

[[[[[but think, to confiscate the dying
of an individual has yet to be done! What
kind of subversion could manage to
surpass such a limit, this absolute limit ...

[for an individual's passage from the
world of confluence, continuity,
along a lived-in perpetuity ...

] what could ever
surpass this?

AND VANISHES (STAGE 6)

A stage, illuminated. A stage, cast in neutrality.

A possible chair – therein.

LUMINOUS

So the earth's secrecy
then be concluded [[through
striations of event,
vanishing into parsed collusion
cause and alterity [by
which the earth acting
accordingly, might speak
of precedent hesitation
]]]] coming to
characterize the nature of its regret
through proximity

[[[the futurity of my discourse
bends [[[and vanishes]
you wanted the world to die (in you)
did the door open?
[you wanted this excision to fade]]]]]
did the door open? this desirous
implication concedes [[[[[didn't you
see yourself
opening the door?
your world in this impossible
collusion of forms …]]]]]

The door was already open.

This is my discourse.

OF LILIES (STAGE 7)

A pond. Perhaps on a smaller scale, a drainage chute. If all are present, each must account its waters to the original source with regularity.

LUMINOUS

Preceding you]]]]]]
Death is what I strew! Death
was yours to despise]]]] in a decisive
agony of lilies – divine galleries of
deathless flora [divinities]]]] death is
what was sown in the fragile, lived
summary of exterior [[[[in
melodic galleries of antecedence]. But this
is something to be certain of. As the meek
bridge mentioned –
something would have come before [[[
had made me awaken to this bent
world] it was,
effectively, yours to despise ...

and from these seeds a consensual
format emerged
as from beneath [a figure
renewed, a figure filled/established in a
gradient of colour, a figure written under
duress]]]]] Numb figure! Unable
to body sensation [[[[[
such a dull figure of chance, she (this
figure) is!] for certain, the
memory's figure is at fault, but all else
remains
intact
[If anything, she is formidable]]]]]
and born from a
consensual seed.

AREAS OF EFFORTLESS AFFRONT UPON THE SAME ASHEN STAGE OF OCCURRENCE (STAGE 8)

Delivery room. Hardwood is being applied by men whose faces remain indistinct. Gypsum alienates the mouth.

LUMINOUS

This dream won't allow my tenderness –
what should I do? [[[Won't accept any
unbelonging moment, undesired]]]
Whose restless anteriority replies across
the marooned instance of its divide.
[[[Spectral confidences across
thatched, sunlit surfaces,]
a tin sound
of spectrality ...

– from the tireless lane, bordered in lilies

a sensual format arose –

– the tireless
lane bordered in lilies and the relevant
disclosures therein [Extract! Extract
the bridge from this swerving materiality!

Divide it.]]]]]

BLANK FILLIGREE GLOVES OF INTENT (STAGE 9)

These mortal charges of law, adrift in thought or a dream ...

LUMINOUS

Dear ... how shall I proceed in this
unmitigated forgiveness?
The longing for renewal bends me.
I am an opal desirousness
under tension [[[this longing for
renewal spites me!] Oh, I can't tell you
how I suffer! And yet, a continually
forgiven dream reunites me with a
salvation that threatens to absolve
me from you – [[[how I've
suffered!]]]

From all that is risen upon this articulate
weave, I sign to you dear,
uncontested flesh [your memory
is still my incomplete
dream]]]

You must know it ...

I MISREMEMBERED (STAGE 10)

A catalyst accounts for change.

LUMINOUS

As for how the whining garden expelled
me, I misremembered.   I had found a
new home in repellent gardens of wasted
foliage!

Alongside evidence of a lifelong tendency
towards preservation, I wasted new seeds
[[beneath fragile ground
      [insisted   the ground
was good   ]]]] The ground was good,
      repealing stones of unmitigated
beginnings –   [as I had manifested
my escapism in stolen agony ...   ]]]]
                                           [
      For now,   death
is in your hands!]]]]]   death's
hands,

POTENTIAL CLARIFICATIONS (STAGE 11)

A looking without object. Appearance is cast in mystery, surface, gauze.

LUMINOUS

[I.e., the sensual chatter of ascent.
I.e., the manner by which the inevitable

would replicate itself, envious of the
singularity it was composed of
wherein dying [houses being]]]]] but
is not a home [[[[[

, I told myself without
conviction, depicting myself in a series of
interchanges all having the potential to
confuse negation with assent] all
having the potential to clarify –

I.e., the shattered glass of a tinted sky.
I.e., the particular darkening of this day.

I.e., the dark breakage of this day.
I.e., the tinted exhaustion of the sky.

Wherein.]

THIS BEAUTY HAS BEEN CAST AFIELD (STAGE 12)

The derailed permissiveness of an unknotted carpet. As of yet, one remains incapable of moving backwards in the passageway.

LUMINOUS

[In a deeply withheld beauty]]]]
– rubbed raw [[[[burnished beyond
resemblance] Fallen between decisive
agonies of loneliness, retraction,
separation – through
repealed distances we became unable to
circumvent – [[[[not even in
dream!]

[not even in dream]]]]]
wherein the same passage became
replicated ... [[[[to have thought it could be
navigated with the same freedom
and irreverence (Falsity!)] Even in
the dream we were unable to become fully
convinced –
in a deeply withheld spontaneity
in the dream, [[[[if this passage

arose] had arisen.

AS NEWS OF THE SPECTACLE REACHED ME, I RETURNED MY FACE TO A SEMBLANCE OF DESIRE SO AS NOT TO BE EXPELLED FROM THE WHINING GARDEN (STAGE 13)

The coal breeze of climate discolours an interior (we are not remiss to mention the remoteness of this enormity).
Solidity encounters a breeze, now rid of exterior. The breeze transcribed now acts as a measure of resemblance.
The breeze now beneath itself, now possessive of reassurance, now cooling to the brow (a relief).

The breeze turns into memory (is replete).
The breeze turns into a fold (is replete).

LUMINOUS

[
In spectacle –   the news reached me:
    an agony of filaments edited their limit
beneath the cold sun, becoming legible as
exterior   [in the sense that they
concealed me in defaced proximity, I
could read appearance   into a defiance
of extent.]]]]   In a sense, I could
not doubt the true secrecy of its decay.
    This corner of discourse decried
willingly ...   I believed in it
so tryingly   [buried in lilies, I was! Their
defeated accumulations   a
particulate wrath]]]]
    and bruised the setting hue of my skin
    [[[a desperate clause defaced]

                                        and their
desperate stamens strewn ...

IT IS NOT WITHIN MY TENDENCY TO MOVE NEGLIGENTLY THROUGH STORMS OF APPEARANCE (STAGE 14)

A picture has been relegated to a corner beyond which encounter establishes a code. The present container of identity repents. The present container of identity is a traversable scale.

As image resolves through chemical fluidity, so the face devolves into action. A picture has now been established.

LUMINOUS

[If I felt that there might have been an [
    before me
there might have been no [there
in actuality, the [was a picture I had
seen accidentally –

The [was a picture and I was there
also, in the picture
and what I remembered of the scene was
not present in that moment
and therefore had no relevance to the
picture

When I look at the picture what I see
is that there is someone there
in the picture
and after that person there is an [there

I feel that this [might be in the picture
or it might be in me
and the person in the picture also
she might be in the [or she might be
in me   ]

A MOMENT BELIED (STAGE 15)

The rising of an operatic stage. Appearance renews its contract with illusion. Visible: a hem of raw silk, its chemical perplexity establishing a growth of mouth or eyelid or cheekbone.

LUMINOUS

The disappearance of an elliptical nerve
(in daylight,   that such
unawareness might pause   in the shade
of its useless unbecoming   )   casting
the tenor of continuance upon exterior –

    [[[[Chance disallowed an imitative
pulse   across whose wideness
emerged an enraged   state of
dereliction]   now this
defenceless change softens and repeals
impossible theatrics.   [[[[
Risking territory or response –

    rain] rain, as it fell with a more
distinct forgiving –

rain] is where
I found my name]

beneath increasing   accumulations
of water   [and lost
                my name once more.]]]]]

V

LOCUTIONARY DIFFERENTIATIONS

❋ FAILED REQUISITE ❋ THE THUNDER PERCEIVED OUTSIDE THE DREAM CONSTITUTING THE THUNDER OCCURING INSIDE ❋ DISCRETE VEIL, VEINED ❋ A GARDEN ❋ SOLELY ❋ STAGE ❋ PORTAL ❋ SERIOUSNESS AND AN ABSENCE OF DRESSES ❋ LUCENT CATEGORIES BENDING BENEATH THE WILLPOWER OF MOONS ❋ NOT THAT SUCH A QUEEN OR WITNESS MIGHT ARISE ❋ THIS CAST SHADOW IS IRRETRIEVABLE ❋ SENSORIUM (BEYOND WHICH WE COUNTER OUR IMPERFECT LIGHT) ❋ THAT THE STAGE BECAME A DESCRIPTION OF THE ROOM, AND ALL IT CONTAINED ❋ ENIGMATIC CINEMAS OF CONTINUTIES UNKNOWN (IT RAINS, VOTIVELY) ❋ MY WORTH, SUSTENANCE, AND RESOLVE ❋ DEFINITION OF TERMS ❋ STARS (A CACOPHONY OF MORAL LAMINATION) ❋ MNEMOSYNE

FAILED REQUISITE

This surpassing which recalls the world.

This world … a requisite surpassing of itself.

ANTI-CHORUS

The birds are flying
again in this way …

I received you

♪ Why do they?

I received you

I am turning | I received you beyond | away from this path,
the birds are | the terms of a possible storm (| flying again in this way …
Across the terms of any
I don't know | probable storm | when I began hearing them,
CHORUS in this | | way becoming aware of new
sensation |) I received …

and the sameness
of all | As this came to pass, | other things.
and birds felled necessity,
I ended | in this way, | the war with resistance
(mine),
it ended then in | the architectural emptiness of | me.
the dream paired its song
with intentionality and surface

♪ I | | won't see you any longer –
will this | and it came to pass that I was to | be?
receive you

CHORUS
I | upon the terms of an | am a ruin that wants time to
disappear, | itinerant dream …
yet where | | would I be without it?

ANTI-CHORUS
We | | desire to destroy,
which can be
destroyed –

CHORUS
♪ Where | | will I be? ♪

THE THUNDER PERCEIVED OUTSIDE OF THE DREAM CONSTITUTING THE THUNDER OCCURING INSIDE

It has rained. Routine likeliness falls from the face, expelled as tears.
The stage is beginning to slip, revealing red-clay topsoil.
It rains, it has rained, it's always raining, here where enormity ages alongside circumference.

In the unmanaged midst, I picture your embodiment as follows:

Clay degrading into grass,
into down, into musk,
silica.

LUMINOUS
The following exchange takes place in rapid succession.

HEROINE
The thunder inside the dream was occurring outside of the dream.

LUMINOUS
This exchange lessens in feverish response.

CHILD
The thunder outside the dream constituted the thunder which was heard inside.

LUMINOUS
This exchange qualifies its response.

HEROINE
While both dreams remained dissimilar, each having the unfinished quality of a setting only partially able to be recalled, somehow the cyclic tenor of thunder remained the same.

LUMINOUS
This exchange solidifies its perfume.

CHILD
The thunder outside the dream attached itself to my sleeping form.

LUMINOUS
This exchange inclines.

HERONE

I beheld it as a beautiful grass dress of silk chiffon.

LUMINOUS

This exchange, soon destroyed.

CHILD

I adorned myself in dream as thunder approached me anew, before passing.

LUMINOUS

This exchange slowly reaches its end.

HEROINE

I fell asleep beneath a tree and beheld it, doubly holding me within and being withheld by my perceiving.

CHILD

I withheld thunder from the distraction of the skies.

HEROINE and CHILD

(*together*) I withheld it from the envy of the stars.

CHILD

How could I have told you?

LUMINOUS

Excise it!

Enter MATERNAL LOVE.

MATERNAL LOVE

At last, in the dream, I held you. You, your revolving surface, and all else that remained. You were present there, in the dawn, you were present in mourning excision, in defaced indifference, you were there, and I loved you as you were, then, in the dawn, in the morning, in the bent honesty of your dereliction.

You were my beautiful child.

Exit MATERNAL LOVE.

HEROINE

How will duration's imbalance carve its outline into the essence of that which has no face? In the semblance of a reflection I do not gaze upon, light refracts from some originary source. The light is cool (if not silver, then a mercurial substitute from which light both gathers and emotes), and while what it illuminates has not yet become visible to me, I recognize it as familiar and embrace it as my own.

LUMINOUS
(*in brocade*)

HEROINE
I want to ensure you'll recognize me, whatever form I may choose to take. I want to enclose you in your face – this is what you have attempted to do to me.

Even when you're not there, I'm able to cast presence outwards from memory, in this way recomposing your face in the midst of your absence.

LUMINOUS
(*in embroidery*)

HEROINE
It's certain that my face has recomposed many other faces in this manner, having met and altered in this way each consensual gaze. Whose face will appear tomorrow? Will it still be mine?

It's certain that, tomorrow, this face will resemble another's.

Enter MATERNAL LOVE.

LUMINOUS
(*in weft*)

MATERNAL LOVE
Time is appearing.

Exit MATERNAL LOVE.

DISCRETE VEIL, VEINED

The distinction is part of the veil.

CHORUS (*azure*)

We closed our windows
and let the snow fall between us,

and undressed and let it fall between us
until we grew cold
and fell asleep.

It's sufficient that you've left this
garden for me to tend.

ANTI-CHORUS

CHORUS

♪ What could you
ever want from such a thing?

To let the snow fall,
closing our windows against it.

ANTI-CHORUS

♪ What is it you might
harbour
within such a thing?

CHORUS

To satisfy all material,
turning our windows to it

ANTI-CHORUS

♪ … such a thing …

A season of rain
Beyond which no circumstance
Likewise descends

While we closed ourselves to
the windows
These scenic contingencies
continued to doubt
And degrade in sensorial lieu

And the season of rain
changed, and the season of rain
was altered, and as a season,
the rain no longer fell, and yet
it remained a season of rain,
though there was no rain, and
the season of rain withheld its
distraction and still the season
could not give forth for rain,
though we did not change its
designation.

Likewise descends, a season
without rain

Became born of the season of
rain

A GARDEN

All structured as follows:

Hibiscus (caged), roses (caged), sage (uncaged), brambles (uncaged), bluets (uncaged), lotus (uncaged), unnamed wildflowers (uncaged, precious), bleeding hearts (caged), sugar cane (encased in plastic, precious), lilies (encased in plastic, precious), tomatoes (encased in plastic), sweet peas (vines arranged over a clothesline, previous).

HEROINE, CHILD, and MATERNAL LOVE

(*singing tonelessly, in repentance*) Our feet once composed (conquered) the passageway between circumstance and fate, our eyes once qualified the tenor of musical phrases both existing and not, our predisposition to cave beneath the extremities of violence became a structural fault whose imaging would resemble kaleidoscopic morphologies.

These are the denied embodiments which began to ossify, turning cold upon our cheeks, darkening our hair with recombinatory parlance.

Exit MATERNAL LOVE.

HEROINE

That any loveliness be shorn by the litmus of regenerative potential –

CHILD

That the continued phase of mimicry be expelled, this intolerable about-face dissociated from itself –

HEROINE

I was given to an operatic voice, a wordless glaze of affect.

Enter MATERNAL LOVE.

MATERNAL LOVE

All true surface has been relegated to continuity.

LUMINOUS

All true breadth.

Exit MATERNAL LOVE.

HERONE

In a blindly (blindingly) distant disturbance of evil, I began to encounter your face: that which was already inscribed upon the passageway.

CHILD

This lovely, unawarded sensation.

HEROINE

Then, any loveliness which may be shorn to reveal its indeterminacy (intolerably coherent, stifled).

CHILD

I was foreign to the enclosed surface.

LUMINOUS

I was bound to a glaze of correspondence.

HEROINE

I was forgiven to this world.

Spotlight falls, elementally.

SOLELY

All structured as follows:

A building (faded, human), a category (implied, inhuman), a decanter (recognizable, human), love (undefined, human or non-human).

A shadowing of assemblage begets a world of potential in which the apparent image comes to be believed, thought of, suggested by means of its own distinction, withdrawn from belief as from memory or witness, supplanting innumerable refractions into unresisting survival –

This constituting seduction.

CHORUS

Any nail, look – any hook.

ANTI-CHORUS (*ethereal*)

As we fail before the
moon,
you, in turn, fail
before us.

ANTI-CHORUS

There is a nail withstanding a hook
There is a hook which withstands a
nail –

Any nail, look – any hook.

Inside, a
flower,
A climb.
As we
might …

STAGE

I allowed the silence of this world to guide me.
I allowed the silence of this world to pass.

Spotlight falls, exceedingly. LUMINOUS is not present on the stage.

Enter MATERNAL LOVE.

HEROINE, CHILD, and MATERNAL LOVE

As the character of our focus came to renew its indifference, so did the nature of our offerings begin changing to include the shadowing of a nebulous vine diverting the pale phrasing of lather collecting over childhood's broad banks, recomposing infrequent remittances of a short-wave broadcast into bird calls, and so the nature of our offerings came to include to include the ceased renewal of a door unable to be reopened once closed; came to include a periphery of hesitation; came to include a formulaic incapacity to alter, reduce, or erase the already occurring dream-event; came to include in its countenance the disobedience of age which would alter and bend the space between passivity and decay in such a way that the face would never again regain its elasticity or the mindlessness of its flawless persuasion; came to include the revival of past behaviour such that the main character loses any capacity for critical self-interrogation, therefore becoming unable to revert to a time before behaviour had ossified into habit; came to include ossification as method of intolerance, ossification as method of self-destruction, ossification as a form of self-love, ossification as a kind of makeup that could be pressed into the face and décolletage.

(*singing tonelessly*)

A provision of tiles, satin, and skin

A variable reconstitutes anticipation

To readjust, wholly, the circumstances of your conviction

To partake in revenue and doubt

To habituate.

Spotlight falls, strenuously.

PORTAL

Cold remainder, occluded!

CHORUS (*defeatedly*)

Alteration occurs
upon a path
of deficiency

Such a notion,
itself uninvolved
with superimpositions
of renewal

Unevolved, implicit:
That the edges of any
posture might inhabit
universality at the far
reaches of its composure

(Repeat
)

at the far edges
of enclosure
(retreat
)

ANTI-CHORUS

Effort: ♪ Now filled.
♪ Now emptied.

Only once exhumed by daylight,
only once sustained by chance:

CHORUS

♪ Now filled.
♪ Now emptied.

The trajectory over which the desired drift
of a current passes (will then pass).

ANTI-CHORUS

Seasonally:

♪ A threshold. ♪

SERIOUSNESS AND AN ABSENCE OF DRESSES

What is the modern equivalence of a disbelieving storm?
"To live through a perennial disfiguration, bound to a disbelieving gaze."

To you, appearance must align with a vitality consigned to surface. No longer.
"Longer? Did you move me, in those days?"

Together, might impossibility have induced an effaceable route?
"Here, we tread an indelible route."

HEROINE, LUMINOUS, and CHILD

(*singing tonelessly*) Ossification is any part of a body that may be recombined to produce another. Ossification is any part of a body that makes one essentially anticipated by those who might encounter it. Ossification is any part of a body that might be suggestive in a way it did not intend. Ossification, or to cave beneath violence in a structured way, is to force certain continuities to become manifest.

CHILD

And what was left but a kind of shell encompassing what had once carried within it infinite variation, disclosure, which had once delimited motivation with the ease of a sharpened blade passing through what wanted to be rent, through what had softened through an eternity only hoping to be divided, to be cut from itself:

(*singing*)
To be split.
To be cloven.

HEROINE

There are whims I shall never dedicate myself to, gardens, which shall never begin to differ.

LUMINOUS

Though one might attempt to uncover ...

HEROINE

There are whims I shall never dedicate, dresses which have not yet begun their suffering.

LUCENT CATEGORIES BENDING BENEATH THE WILLPOWER OF MOONS

Adjust your purview to include the moment's physical irrelevancies – a slight (unnoticed) breakage in the continuity of a visage whose veracity relies upon a precedent betrayal. To contain the transposed legibility of the face, to compose, be witness to, depart from, be renewed in awareness of this fragility is a betrayal which cannot be surpassed.

To rehearse in dialogic relation (back slightly arched, braced in effacement) – the essence of this indifference is multiple.

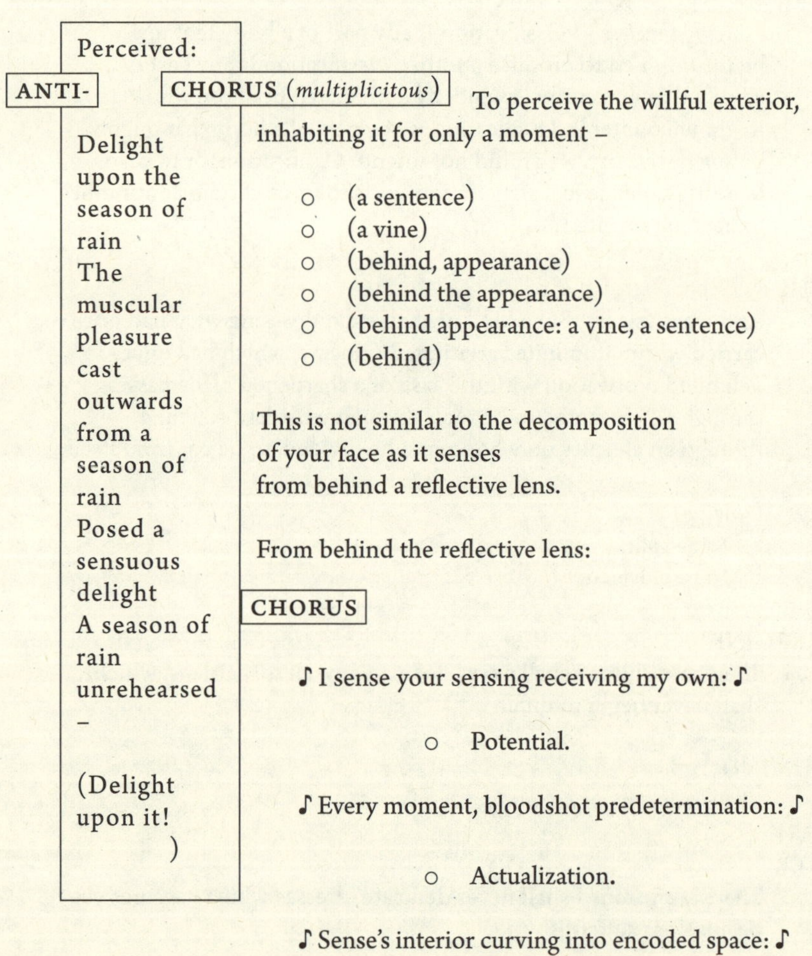

Perceived:

ANTI-

CHORUS (*multiplicitous*)

Delight
upon the
season of
rain
The
muscular
pleasure
cast
outwards
from a
season of
rain
Posed a
sensuous
delight
A season of
rain
unrehearsed
–

(Delight
upon it!
)

To perceive the willful exterior, inhabiting it for only a moment –

- (a sentence)
- (a vine)
- (behind, appearance)
- (behind the appearance)
- (behind appearance: a vine, a sentence)
- (behind)

This is not similar to the decomposition
of your face as it senses
from behind a reflective lens.

From behind the reflective lens:

CHORUS

♪ I sense your sensing receiving my own: ♪

- Potential.

♪ Every moment, bloodshot predetermination: ♪

- Actualization.

♪ Sense's interior curving into encoded space: ♪

- Appearance.

NOT THAT SUCH A QUEEN OR WITNESS MIGHT ARISE

The limit of a dream is not that which recomposes itself in fragile physicality. Not that which reminisces upon perfection, prismatic in its variegation, variable as innumerable locks of hair, as unbodied desirousness, as inane obsession.

The limit of a dream is not that which comprehends the boundary between possibility and contempt. The boundary of the dream indicates its contempt through locale. Between passivity and its recombination with logic: the fact that such a limit exists.

HEROINE

Upon the design of a perceiving body, I plant the remains of a seed which does not yield.

LUMINOUS

Why have you planted it?

CHILD

The shade unearths itself to sun.

HEROINE

In darkness you want to live your life, unseen.

LUMINOUS

Your depth humiliates the substance of growth.

CHILD

In a jar on the counter there are rosebuds which have dried to a tincture. Roses occur often, but I still don't know why.

HEROINE

There is intimacy. Paired substance.

Enter MATERNAL LOVE.

MATERNAL LOVE

With space appearing too vast, thought becomes unable to damage action's thin filament. For thought to be enacted, there needs to be an edge against which process can occur.

Exit MATERNAL LOVE.

LUMINOUS

Passage before the reverie, wind causing fissures to pulsate within its shadow.

Enter MATERNAL LOVE.

MATERNAL LOVE

This isn't so much a recital of intention as it is an interchange between desire and the material substance of its past.

Exit MATERNAL LOVE.

LUMINOUS

Violate!

THIS CAST SHADOW IS IRRETRIEVABLE

Tiered projections of sensuality.

	Occurrent upon the exceedingly	**CHORUS** (*inevitably*)
	visible plane:	
	Striations of causality	Alongside an undifferentiated
	hardening defeatedly	path,
	over disclosure	we encounter, or look away.
♪	The inevitability	You look away,
♪	by which a series of suns continued	undoing the road,
♪	to bend into time, recanting all	undoing the gaze,
	previous iterations of daylight	
believing		the singularity of this passage
will pass.	By which the efficacy of an original	
	design (in a sense, its continuity,	
♪		When did I start answering
	) might relate itself	to finitude?
	in fictive essence	
When I	To any possible combination	became aware of myself.
	of return;	
♪	possible futurity …	When did I become aware of
		myself?
	The posited supposition of any path	
When the	arising therein,	sad absence of the stranger took
my place.	the past's defeated recollection	
	which retreats so far as to be scarcely	
♪	visible (as emanation)	What did this sensation entail?
	distant (as distinction	
All I had	) as any separable force	become unable to touch or part
	between material, matter and	from remaining indifferently at
	currency,	my side.
	surface and collusion,	
As that	transparency and occlusion –	which might assure me of
		sameness,
a	or the possibility of any other	cumulative dimming of stars,
	combination	
♪	existing therein.	and all else this entails. ♪

SENSORIUM (BEYOND WHICH WE COUNTER OUR IMPERFECT LIGHT)

A shadowed (shadowing) sensorium.

LUMINOUS is not present on the stage.

CHILD and HERONE

(*singing*)

Look, the leaves.
Look, the deveined faces.
Look, roads parting to grass (beloved).
Look (a world).

Enter MATERNAL LOVE.

MATERNAL LOVE

As a word might begin its inordinate, willful transit within abandonment ...

CHILD

The cooling of the night.

MATERNAL LOVE

Its breakage.

HEROINE

Though sleep rarely participates, words within the dream clatter like dishes at eventide.

CHILD

Where has the bottle-green notion of desire relocated? Has it burrowed into new flesh, long departed?

MATERNAL LOVE

At times I manage to love you more, less at others.

CHILD

Discovering you in the delirium of your despair, I became bodied in it, invoking a gross sentencing of remorse, seeding myself in the tacit envy of its complexion.

HEROINE

It was you who had seeded it in me, perversely allowing roots to grow and emerge into visibility, becoming inseparable from any system that might have allowed its escape.

Exit MATERNAL LOVE.

Enter MATERNAL LOVE.

MATERNAL LOVE

Context, in its surfacing, may now solder a more forgiving countenance.

Exit MATERNAL LOVE.

CHILD

I stopped to record the movement occurring in the midst of a storm, a storm of frailty and immersion.

HEROINE

Now furthering resemblance through past exterior –

CHILD

A storm of encounter, wrathful.

HEROINE

Why do you always water your gardens with such abandon? You will die!

THAT THE STAGE BECAME A DESCRIPTION OF THE ROOM, AND ALL IT CONTAINED

A limit is expressed.
A limit becomes manifest.
A limit is drawn, bordered, animated.

The passage of air through a limit is circumstantial.
The notation of limit into figure or intuition
is kinesis establishing new and fateful currents of concern.

The quietude of the air establishes my remorse.
Quiet circumstance caters itself to the same.
This trespass encounters.

ANTI-CHORUS

	The light, without its required	
You	agency, without its rapidity	wanted the persistent root
of history ...	Exists as the world does and is	
	recognizable within the world	
		♪ Repealed in
	That the wound in its agency	transactional descent.
	departs from its subject	
You	(This world which ages those	wanted the rain to fall ...
	who are in it)	
		♪ As it would have.
	Without such disuse	♪ As it might have
descended, then.	Without such hesitation	
You	What the world ages	wanted the world to seal
remorse,	in exceeding indiscretion	
	And vanishes	♪ to solidify in a state
of abjection.	And reveres	
But	While there exists no matter beyond	still a season would pass,
	the closed and contingent sun	
	A linguistic grammar of forms	♪ then giving way to
formulaic	forcefully reveals a subject	resemblance.
And	O seed!	still another world
	O my struggle!	would pass.

ENIGMATIC CINEMAS OF CONTINUTIES UNKNOWN (IT RAINS, VOTIVELY)

Intimacy upon a collective scale. Filial, a route which contests excursion. The flattened contextuality of a room whose weft is possessive of discourse. Event stills to a Technicolor focus.

CHILD is not present on the stage.

Enter MATERNAL LOVE.

MATERNAL LOVE

Determination's prior locale relaxes its anterior musculature only under one condition – that this determination be easily surpassed by a more fitting condition (should such a requisite happen to come along).

Exit MATERNAL LOVE.

HEROINE

One might have been passing over the bridge to one's childhood, a fair bridge, too small perhaps, for one's current size (sturdy nonetheless) ...

LUMINOUS

Dream, dreamed without outline.

HEROINE

Daylight does not ebb as it once did.

Enter MATERNAL LOVE.

MATERNAL LOVE

I called upon you to witness the traces of occasion preceding my passage into debasement. Now a singular structure composed of rapidity, enclosure, anticipation. Enclosed in an office of probability, the causality of encounter is a tempting orifice (protrusion) I might cast myself against, within, or beyond.

LUMINOUS

The facet of a weight bending beneath circuitous refraction, differentiating ...

MATERNAL LOVE

An edifice (stonewashed, human).
A chalice (recognizable, human).
A catalyst (unrecognizable, immanent).

LUMINOUS

Amid fractured accumulations, your unremitting gaze ...

HEROINE

Wasted ... everything wasted ...

MATERNAL LOVE

To think too deeply is an ignorance. Why have you purged me from your material belonging? Why do you repent?

Exit MATERNAL LOVE.

LUMINOUS

Sensed beneath the bridge's facticity.

HEROINE

You've left behind (abandoned) the face I used to hold, yet I haven't forgotten it. It isn't what you see – but since when have you been able to see what is there, when it is there?

Enter MATERNAL LOVE.

MATERNAL LOVE

Many times had I injured the mask, following the site of injury to its corresponding space of concealment as one might follow an animal to its lair. Its atmosphere was seasonally in decline. Change occurred in a rapid sequence of effects. As my surroundings transformed, I found myself adorned in a variance previously unknown to me: now an emblem with shorn hair, now an emblem with sliced eyes, now with impossible teeth, now hair allowed to grow needlessly in an excess of meaning. At times, a characteristic imperfection, a sneer, making the mask that much more compelling (decipherable) to all who came to gaze upon it.

Exit MATERNAL LOVE.

HEROINE

Her/My desirous adornment took the place of the/my body.
She/I was a beautiful (needless) potential.

And then autumn would return.
And then beauty would fall from me.

MY WORTH, SUSTENANCE, AND RESOLVE

Both legible and infinitely illegible, a perceptible face has the capacity to be inscribed (but never with indelible ink).

CHORUS

The clouds are such an idle
abbreviation

I replicate
a system as
diverse as myself
And with
as much as that
system might
require

How should I have
expected you,
equally strange in
transience,
opened to myself,
anew?

Here, I
manifest a relative sensation:

I am both afraid
of
continue.

I am always forgetting

of time repeating,
continuing and failing to

There is a
distance

ANTI-CHORUS

Here, I manifest
a relative sensation:

I am both afraid
of time repeating and of it
failing to repeat

Those
beginnings in some
And all

Of continuing
and failing to continue

It continues

things which have their
end.
things whose beginnings
were born –

CHORUS

This
is finitude's perfect nature.

Both this,

and its breakage.

DEFINITION OF TERMS

Recall:	*Finitude expresses a name.*
The root:	*Clouded origination.*
The dream:	*Depletion upon a year.*
Firmness:	*Fertility of sequence.*
Untrue passages:	*Fate.*
Constructed remarks:	*An exterior of resemblance or shame.*
Fate:	*Decision.*

HEROINE

As might a star stretch, then retract. With inevitability, its skin growing cold. Consider the gaze which fastens us at a distance. Every trace of myself, perhaps inadvertently shed, may come to counter your hands.

I picture our bodies meeting beneath the inevitability of force. I imagine our bodies parting in this way.

Enter MATERNAL LOVE.

MATERNAL LOVE

Inevitability may transfer motive onto any existing body – this is its rule.

Exit MATERNAL LOVE.

HEROINE

As a mountain might part its path of resemblance.

CHILD

A rule. A return to the plausibility of encounter.

HEROINE

Look. To see a star is to love. Can this be called human?

Enter MATERNAL LOVE.

MATERNAL LOVE

As death hesitates to renew growth, I am as I am; figurally disappointed.

CHILD

I am as I am.

Exit CHILD.

MATERNAL LOVE

Inevitability. The slow, grazing exclusion whose semblance is subtraction. How is it to be verified by addition? How then, to acquire through failure, to agitate?

HEROINE

To align?

MATERNAL LOVE

To agitate.

HEROINE

To have vanished in the process of forging your own trail ...

MATERNAL LOVE

As of yet, an unimaginable terrace.

Exit MATERNAL LOVE.

STARS (A CACOPHONY OF MORAL LAMINATION)

Stars are sung with limit. Stars are bordered in offence (aflame), bound by perversity (alight). Stars are afterthoughts, renewing locally through a single, sustaining limit.

A star is just a grievous omission.

Inimitable are stars sung with gratitude. Inimitable stars now are being sung. Repellent are stars sung in terror. Repellent stars are now being sung.

CHILD, HEROINE, and MATERNAL LOVE are not present on the stage.

CHORUS
(*aflame, singing*) I light the star and all I am able to see
gazes equally into me.

ANTI-CHORUS
This star outlives perspective.

CHORUS
(*singing*) I set the star aflame and all I am able to see
gazes equally into me.

ANTI-CHORUS
This star dims in its relation
with all else that casts its light.

CHORUS
(*singing*) I light the star and all that appears
appears madly within me.

ANTI-CHORUS
I outlive the star!
(I have outlived the star's stark seeming!)

CHORUS
(*singing*) I set this star alight and all that appears
appears madly in me.

LUMINOUS
(*aggrieved*) *I have wasted the effortlessness*
of this gaze beneath the sun!

MNEMOSYNE

If it is raining, we have already bordered this boundary with resolution. LUMINOUS is not the only star, but one among many others yet to be named.

All characters are present on the stage.

HEROINE

This solitary star whose light I, alone, live by. This star whose inescapable memory overpowers my own. This star whose singularity I'm now capable of forgetting, whose name has been revealed to be: LUMINOUS.

Forgetting has become forgiveness's sole substance.

CHILD

(*struck down*) Drawing you into time, discarding you
into the sun ...

LUMINOUS

I cannot forgive you. It is not my goal to mournfully pre-exist God.

MATERNAL LOVE

Cast her out!

Cast her out!

Cast her out!

Cast her out!

Cast her out!

Cast her out!

Cast her out!

HEROINE, CHILD, and MATERNAL LOVE

(*chanting*) Cast her out!

LUMINOUS

(*wailing*) *In the whole world! The entire thing!*
I haven't found a home in the whole world!

VI

LUMINOUS

The setting, which cannot situationally be called a stage, defies correlation. The closest means of comparison would require an improbable excursion into descriptive colour, the adjacent shadow cast by light being, in material composition, a luminous discovery of laws through which appearance attends to exterior's unshakeable errancies.

LUMINOUS enters wearing a torn slip of light-incising silk.

LUMINOUS
(*singing*) THE SUN APPEARED BEFORE ME

THE SUN APPEARED BEFORE A LONG PATH

I FOLLOWED THE SUN TO ITS COMPLETION

The sun appeared through a vast sense of having slept,
then following me through waking's brooding expanse.

I FORESAW AN IMAGE

I foresaw an image
while contemplating its endlessness,
alone and very far from the dream.

I saw myself paused before
that which I was unable to see …

Many images appeared to me then.

I PAUSED –

From an unmistakable page:
the heat of the sun.

Vague parentheses parting
to a canopy of delight:

Delight surpassed by emptiness.

OTHER PETALS HAVING SIMPLY FALLEN

Furthermore. Lilies still bloomed, though there remained no light by which to see them. While there existed no light by which one might encounter an unperceived image of lilies blooming, the flowers themselves cast a serene light, palely perceptible.

The lilies crossed the night. The lilies, themselves.
The lilies with their indeterminable glance,
the lilies with their powerless glare, the lilies
viewing themselves within the luminosity
of their gaze, itself suggestive of halogen.

OTHER PETALS HAVING CAUSE TO FALL

To again notate:
        a sequence in exceeding miniature

was then to notice
        succession (delimitation).

It was then I began to notice a series in particularity,
        extending outwards,
        beyond an inarticulate plane.

It was then I began to notice
        the ambivalence of stars in exceeding miniature,
        whose dispersal likewise came to arbitrate.

... While what the light of the lilies revealed clarified nothing about the surrounding area, there remained nothing separating what we saw from what we thought we were seeing, both light and dark being clearly delimited in the sense of being opposing forces, neither the light nor dark being capable of revealing what existed outside of the space the lilies were in, outside the space we were also in, outside of the light, outside ...

IT WAS A LONG PATH

IT'S ALWAYS A LONG PATH

You are as abstract as this room,
as the dream within itself.

OTHER PETALS HAVING HAD CAUSE TO FALL

Of course, the moonlight was a chance demeanour.

Of course, we failed to notice it, how and when

the night might have crossed moonlight

with a similar effect upon a coeval trajectory.

Of course, we were unbeknownst to the particularities,

as unwillingness came to resemble our certainty.

We had been unknown to the particularities,

hesitant.

OTHER PETALS HAVING FALLEN IN SIMULTANEOUS EXCRETION

By then, the moon having abandoned itself within the tranquility of a room, having abandoned within itself any hesitancy to enact change, abandoning itself within any method of disclosure otherwise presumed –

By then, the moon having abandoned itself within a tranquility of reference, having been expunged, receiving adequate attentions and nourishment, then giving way to petals which would fall and scatter in a breeze –

OTHER PETALS HAVING CEDED TO A RECOMMENDATION OF EFFECT

… Even then, the means by which wind intersected a bodily conviction, positioned beneath the gilded shield of witness, even then, knowing the wind exactly as I had known it then, even then, forcing sound to acquiesce in a solution of exterior, even then, knowing the wind had even more substance than I, even then, knowing all I was to continue knowing, even then …

OTHER PETALS CONTINUED TO FALL

To this anterior moon I have returned,
among the fragmentation of its halo.

In a sense, this moon.
In a sense, this halo.

Among diverse corrections of matter,
it is to this moon I have returned,
discarding a series to the effect of feverish renewal.

I EXPECT THE DREAM IS ALSO SUCH AN INCLUSIVE SPACE

Containing no true necessity
                    through rain which had damaged
                    contingent surfaces with a present survival,
                    whose surfacing would pool indelibly
                    over the relative unfeeling of the ground,
                    over the relative unfeeling of the surface I was
                    becoming –

                    over the petal, which unflowing,
                    shed the exterior of its excess

                    and interior of the same,
                    so it was in such a way
                    that excess became intimacy,

                    pooling over the excess of the body,
                    pooling over the survival of the earth
                                                            itself covered, unfeeling,

feeding discretely
over petals which had unfurled over the course
of countless consecutive nights,
over the wind and the landscape,
over the breathless receptivity of all those
who find themselves incapable of speech
after a long and routed deception –

AFTERWARDS

EVEN AFTERWARDS, AS ADDITIVE OF THE WIND'S SUCCESSION

EVEN AFTERWARDS, AS FILAMENT

EVEN AFTERWARDS, AFFRONT

... Afterwards, wind wove exceedingly through the character of my silence. Its singularity was calm, silken, suggestive with brocade, protracted.

The wind then wove through as a characterization of my silence. I encountered no resistance as my gaze fell year after year upon this or any other thing, nor did any resistance befall those whose gaze afterwards encountered mine.

Nor did I befall anyone whose gaze encountered me,
nor did any resistance befall those whose gaze encountered them.

Even afterwards, the wind imposed its relative permanence,
imbuing surface with a precision coeval to cause.

EVEN AFTERWARDS ...

Is the emptiness of the door (object) alight?
Are the figures in the image (door) impartially lit?

The trees were decisively discordant,
moonlight eclipsing any trail figure might have made.

I ran across you in the linguistic insolvency of persistence,
beyond whose gaze continued to strain – I ran across you
in the fragmented perusal of existing, I ran into you, frailly –

  Even then,
    the sense of afterwards bodied our parallelism.

INTERIOR CASTS ITS RETROSPECTIVE LIGHT

Where is located the indivisible factor in this continuity
    of perpetual exchange?

The rain is denying any opportunity to revive itself in illusion.

The rain is denying any opportunity to press monument
    into change

While this page returns insolvency to repetition

With futility and silence, we refused to meet –
    but what was it that has returned to us?

Was it illusion?

IT OCCURS TO ME THAT I AM LOST

WHY AM I LOST?

I failed a dream in reversal, derided
  myself to an odd glow in the sky.

Traditionally, I had asked for nothing
  as all things surpassed me.

I awoke to this morning of sustenance

  (my specialty being

  to bring the stars inside).

The flowers opened and bloomed once before turning.
        While all of it occurred inside of abundance ...

The synchronicity of thunder occurring among the stars

        (which are

        outside).

I HAD BELIEVED IN A SPATIALITY OF EXCEPTION

WHY WAS I LOST?

With the discrete determinism of a flower risen to fall,
        I fell into an eventual mannerism of decay.

The evening cools to a surfactant dream
        the coded relations of time in turn composing themselves
        as iterations of cloud and sunlight.

Again, dawn persists behind the clouds
        despite my changed subjectivity,

despite the difference in the age of the woman
        appearing in the foreground of the image

        (now

        redacted).

INTERRUPTION, WILLED INTO FUTURE

WAS I LOST?

The veiled disorder of language
        is a container whose percussive leaking
        reveals only itself

—that is,

whose experiential occlusions coexist
within language's saline hiddenness.

While the spoken comes to assume a liminal
gloss, fertility is marred.

Across appearance's permissive locutions:
an etiquette of survival wherein disappearance
is inadequately defaced.

Arrival, then, must dissolve.

WHERE BOUND TO OCCUR WERE MOUNTAINS OF IRIS

A woman is looking outside a window.
Whose shadow is cast in the background of a room.
You are looking in.
Something intersects the window.
In the front there is this false mimicry.
Whose shadow is cast in the background of a room.
You are looking in.
Whose shadow comes up from the ground.
In the front there's this false mimicry.

MOUNTAINS (DECISIVELY DISCORDANT)

The garden.

The woman.

Something comes up from the ground.
How one returns with one's face
to the outside remains unknown

(how one returns

to one's face).

To again notate:
A series in exceeding miniature.

THE RAIN IS DENYING ITSELF TO US

The suggestive spatiality indifference might incur:
a carefully displaced sun.

So made space for us in this carelessly edited room,
sobbing mathematically.

The interpellations of dawn are a persistence
whose persona dons a mask—

That, in itself, begets a double.
The persistence, the personage, are. Is, chromatic—
The spectral confidences of an intractable (immutable) drive.
To know and agree to the terms of this contract is to broach
an understanding whose bond is reliant upon substance.

But of the excess of the sky, its varied constellations,
refractions, and concealments?

What of the solar stillness?

WHAT OF IT?

I turned inwards, towards irreverent balustrades,
marble buttresses encased in Platonic thought,
bathwater lined in maple, fragility paired with response,
or all implications coeval within.

I turned inwards towards a Technicolor transparency,
wherein light passes through the insolvency of exterior,
passing through to illuminate—what?

This light which appears through future,
incising surface with reflection.

I DREAMED ACROSS A TANGENTIAL BODILESSNESS

A sense in which the past's diffusive echo might come to resemble an equally diffusive alliteration of future, or that future might exist in iteration of a past yet to occur –

WHOSE HISTORY COULD THIS HAVE BEEN?

To return gestural solidities to recognition,

I wept upon a tangential form.

The beginnings of experience:

A darkness,

occlusive.

I spoke only upon tangential terms.

I wrote a rose into boundless territory,

into deathless dramaturgy,

a face in process of repair –

I wrote as history unfolded.

THE SEARING ROAD

You, whose archipelagos don't exist.
You, whose appearing suggests a passing by.

I am saddened that in the dream you are either beloved or not – those terms aren't interchangeable but so they appear (in dream). I have a limited capacity to alter or influence what is seen, but I can't change this aspect of your appearing (in dream) –

When awake, I notice now
I'm dreaming.

THE SHINING ROAD …

There isn't a page beyond this one.

The sun relates its heat to me.

The sky its clarity or occlusion.

There isn't a page beyond this one.

THIS FAILURE, A THINNESS ALLOWING TECHNICOLOR LIGHT TO PASS THROUGH

… I recombined my past without sensation. By then, a diaphanous star had likewise unspun, exhibiting a fine material constitutive of light and temperature. Through timed landscapes of change and discord, through untimely pressures of facticity drawn bodily through falsity, *bodily* …

I turned inwards to reply, "I have not yet moved to change this extant landscape." I had not yet turned to say, "Where we might have left ourselves, surface has taken our place."

Surface has taken the place of where we might have left ourselves.

DUSK SUSTAINED

Dusk insisted upon adornment, it sustained a velvet coat. Covering worn in mindless repetition.

Mindlessness contained, whose sequined embellishments became situated upon sleeve and shoulder.

Only an invisible seam, unadorned in transition between limb and torso, held any true beauty.

The interpellations of dawn were a suggestive manifest.

The indifference of your true appearing held its beauty up to me: a protective, though indifferent, gown.

WHEREIN OBJECTS IMMERSE THEIR RESIDUAL SURFACES

Surface survives my progression (hovers above) –

that which hovers in morning is a pre-arranged sensitivity

hesitant to adorn resplendence with specificity.

Beyond every eventless relation (limitless exterior),

there is a depth whose willpower is a season.

Whose depths are a season (faded).

In the objectivity of your dream, what constitutes (iterates) its objective nature? Are the physical constraints of recognition a veracity predicative of affective response? Where is located the containing factor of any gestural continuity, any sustaining, any exchange?

THE DEEPENING OF SKIES OPENING TO REFERENCE

WHEREIN OBJECTS CAST A PROCEDURAL LIGHT

The roses in appearance are adjusting themselves in a conference of receiving, an unknown they hold in theoretical balance. The roses in appearance are an immanent contradiction.

While the deepening of the skies now and again opens to reference,
    this habit of appearing counters itself
    in consumed muscularity.

WHEREIN OBJECTS CAST AN ABJECT LIGHT

The birds in order of appearance
each withhold their ossifications.

AND EVERY UNBEARABLE GROVE

THE SILK ERA OF ENTANGLEMENT

This unbearable grove.

This life as life expects.

Please be aware of what I require.

I am bending with great possibility upon the thinness of desire.

THE SILK OF DAYLIGHT

The space remaining for light to punctuate the dark,
    the space left in the shadows of dusk,
    this preferential silk
                                                    (of daylight).

AND WITHIN ITS VELVET COAT ...

To write thinly

upon the space of that light

and every unbearable grove.

I BEGAN TO WRITE –

I began to recite what I had written in the dust,
though some of the words had been displaced …

A PROFUNDITY OF EXTERIOR IN THE IMAGE'S
ONLY SURFACE

In an instant withheld, I fed myself to the light of the stars. The minuscule dawn retreated into an oblique impression of those previous while withdrawing any response behind a dim, superficial halo.

Even with a goal in mind,
I hesitated.

SOME OF THE WORDS HAD EXPIRED, SOFTENING IN
DISCOLOURATION

I FED MYSELF TO THE STARS

Can this image even become the sky?
Can the sky become its image?

We coerced ourselves into inhabiting a relative locution:
a circumstantial room at the core of a disappearance.

I FED MYSELF TO THE LIGHT OF THE STARS

TO A MEDIAL SEASONALITY OF EXCHANGE

A GREEN SEASON

A leaf fell downwards,
towards an unknown extremity.

I later learned how to intentionally trim
or harvest a measure of the needed subsistence,
thus ensuring survival of the immediate body
despite the absence of its previous parts.

To desire in abundance
a life which is always changing –

A shadow visited that place again in the future.
And lived there from then on.

Your desire for abundance is an image which remains –
In actuality, such a desire no longer exists in me.

THE ROAD TURNED AWAY

The road turned, a fiction … away.
The fractal road … a fiction,
away.

THAT YOUR REGARD FOR MATTER ALSO BEND

I had been expended by that day in particular.
I wrote to you that day in the garden,

to you in that garden of closure.
To you, in that garden of defeat.
That particular garden whose remains I became partial to.

I've returned to that garden once more.

I had been exalted by that day (

in the garden,

... was left behind.

... took the shape of a flower).

Though the particularity of the flower I could not recall,
I was aware of its contingency
and the bright red through which it appeared
in the externality of which I was a part –

SENSATION TURNED INTO WORDS

BEFORE RESOLVING INTO IMAGE

Continuity requires
that your regard for matter also bend.

THIS, ITS CONSISTENT SURFACE

ITS WEFT

The synchronicity of thunder occurring among the stars

which are complete.

The fallen system of this rain
the remainder of stars cast in revision –

(as exist
among the clouds).

This rain whose fallen persuasion
faults the indifference of all those it falls upon

and the exceeding thinness of that rain in turn.

I extracted a semblance of future from the past.
I celebrated upon the passing of a year.

For when the rain delights
in the sharp resolution which cedes its beginning
through disclosure, that beauty becomes tinted
with sadness from there on.

Upon the passing of a year, I mourned.

Won't the unheld memory of the world,
and seeking of its reference,
ever mark us with its decisive humidity?

This unheld memory of void, this fruitless world ...
This wished-for harm ...

Will it?

THE ONE WHO BELIES TEMPTATION

THE ONE WHOSE BASTION IS A RELATIVE FORGOING

Ambiguities structure the dawn's architectural seeming.

The birds in appearance cast their relative advance.

The birds in paradisal utterance relate themselves to substance,
their dreams to ambiguity.

IS THIS IMAGE ONE OF POTENTIAL?

They, too, dream unerringly beyond dawn's circuitous element
(beyond dawn's elemental radiance).

A DEFEATED SUBJECTIVITY IS LIKENED TO THE RAIN
WHICH FALLS

Though discarded,
the involuntary sound of the room
persisted in unmanageable repetition.

The involuntary sound of the room to this day persists
in unimaginative survival.

I derived myself along a definitive route.

Though clarity was being recalled in the distance,
 it could not be recounted to me.

IT OCCURS TO ME THAT I AM LOST

FAREWELL

FAREWELL TO ALLIANCE

FAREWELL TO THE ODD GLOW IN THE SKY

For us, is there grief?
Is there an unrepeatable room?

 Are you ...

 Farewell?

BEYOND

This beyond which courses from nowhere
 originates from the same unintelligible hand,
 the same mocking tense –

 This beyond.

Such were the favours granted to us by time.

I WANTED TO FATEFULLY FALL AWAY FROM MYSELF

The end of a garden is always that which opens up onto:

 the world, fixture of continuity,
 lined in grass, et cetera.

The end of a garden
is that which opens up onto a world,
a morning
which precedes us,
fictionally,
which is to say, perpetually present in the same way,
in the same reoccurring dream,
the same occurrent end –

To this disguise which extends itself to the movement of the sky,
to the movement of this earth
as it moves in a manner reminiscent of future,

in a manner reminiscent of time …

AM I SEEING UNINHIBITEDLY INTO THIS DREAM?

A certain structural imperviousness
might adjust its limit as required.
A dream might prove to encourage
a previously unrepeatable contestation.

A dream might presume to encourage undeniable growth
or fall into obscurity.

The leaves which might fall implacably across,
assurance then blistering.

A mysteriously approaching tree whose leaves

fall implacably across,

then blistering.

… as for a single moment between dusk and the merging of night where light chose to conceal its absence, marking our distance as absolute. Distance became resolute as connective tissue, addressing itself to the unrepeatable door. Beyond such immersion, I rose to content in its need, its unbearable pressure extending through interior,

through disarray.

AM I SEEING ELSEWHERE INTO THIS DREAM?

I am shocked into seeing the same stars as you do.

I'm shocked into tireless resolution
and in their undeniable place, another immensity.

... beyond such predications I arose, to no aim.

Upon every journey's end, there are carnations.

Is this our unrepeatable moon?

THE GARDEN, THINNED –

THE FLOWERS THEN APPEARED AS I HAD REMEMBERED THEM

With a flourish, the flowers appear as I remembered them. The flowers appeared in essence to be the same flowers I had seen before. A certain familiarity, sensation of parallelism, convinced me that these flowers had occurred once before – that this iteration was, in a way, a route and programmable recurrence.

It's clear that its totality preferred me.

This garden which has collected me to it –

What shall I call it?

I COMPOSED MYSELF IN AN AESTHETIC OF CONTEXTUAL CHANGE

I, too, am wracked with indifference.

What else should I say

of this blatant masquerade?

GORGEOUS GARDENS PROVIDED THEIR GENEROUS FRUIT

WE GORGED OF THE SAME OPULENT MEAL

Gorgeous gardens provided us with an element of fate.
Gorgeous gardens provided us with generous fruit.

... I fell upon an expanse of rain, as willed by the water. The rain fell as I pried it from the clouds, forcing it to reside beneath my fate, it fell into me still, and still I expelled it, for it was what the earth had granted, as did the water accept me as an element of itself, without will or expectation, as I forced matter to change into sorrow, extracting it from the stage into what would become my home, letting it fall through my fingers and subtract itself into the dirt.

EXTRACT IT!

Blending into beatific gardens,
bound and engaged,
I fell upon an expanse of rain

(as willed by the water).

Bend and fell.
Bend and fell,

as witnessed by the water.

GENEROUSLY, GARDENS PROVIDED FOR US

THOUGH WE TIRED OF THEIR UNCHANGED OPULENCE

... I waited many years as my burden became that which fed me, in a way, and as I spoke into the persistence of my surviving, I was able to articulate (in a way) this material of being as it transformed into satiation, and in so doing gardens bloomed with an overwhelming harvest of wheat and corn.

We turned it into our food
and lived many years that way.

Burdening concept with iteration
We set the probability of event alight
Whose glow composed an ulterior continuity

Finally providing us:

    a glance.

OCCLUSION BEING ANOTHER FORM WAITING TAKES

I wrote myself into a thesis of change. I wanted to trace the inevitability of this exchange by way of inquiring after its hiddenness.

Occluded by every relevant surface – another meaning always appeared to take its place.

I am sure this discovery must be followed by another inquiry I have yet to make.

I want everything to reveal something

but nothing ever does.

I wanted everything to reveal something

but nothing ever did –

Beyond the collective storm, rain renews its contract with desire.
Such are the repetitions which remain.

AS FOR HOW THE SKY GROWS DEAFENINGLY DARK, THIS IS ITS SUBJECTIVITY

I spoke on such gradual terms to potentiality

The clouds as such were an unalienable form

Whose gaze yellowed in unbeautiful supposition

I dreamed among a bodiless fixture.

The true featurelessness of your appearance

Causes an indelible name to pass

Just as that which I can neither remember nor return to

The rain conducts this featurelessness.

THE RAIN REPEALS ITS IMAGERY

You whose occupations don't exist

You whose numbness is an overflowing

You whose tenacity is an iterative objectivity

THE DAY WAS COMPOSED OF IT

Your expectation was to remain beloved to all encounter

Whose dreams persisted in ambiguous interlude

EVERY JOURNEY ENDS WITH CARNATIONS

... greeting in exchange a sensorium of my own, offering myself as contractual subject – I became unalike. I revelled in the garden and gained admittance to its unrepeatable moon,

with its leaves and barricades, with a sifted sensuality
whose rows presented its lie in a sidelong glance.

While the same gardens inflict us with submission, in an attitude of renewal I again implemented the garden with gratitude, coerced by the sinister resistance of the stars, the sidelong phrase of their sightlessness.

THE RESISTANCE OF A FACE PRECEDES

IS THIS GRIEF OUR UNREPEATABLE PASTORAL?

My process was systematic.
I consigned myself to a vitality of surface.

Renewal was an emanation – I received it in solitude.

Deciduous roses decanted their subjectivities.

The garden of roses deflating,
having deemed such a presence worthless ...

A worthlessness whose intuition then coloured the skies
With the same devalued glow:

Shades of resolution paired
with an incandescent tint.

YESTERDAY, I SEPARATED FROM RENEWAL

I CRIED UPON A BOUNDLESS FORM

Yesterday, I separated from renewal
and in so doing, damaged a boundless form,
darkening the canopy with disbelief.

These are questions I absorbed
in the suggestive quantity of a room which preceded me –
questions I willed into the room.

These are questions
which I valued as precedents.

I DREAMED IN LIEU OF MY ENVY

OR, DISBELIEF: THE VULNERABLE ENVY OF THE PRESENT

REDUCIBLE, THE PETALS NOW FALLEN

I slept beneath a creased imperfection.

I slept as a container of vice.

I slept … I slept …

What waste, the stars …

It's late afternoon.

Nothing's moving

but the dawn.

FIN

AFTERWORD

SOME NOTES ON LIGHT AND MEMORY

Andy Martrich

At the end of Pier Paolo Pasolini's 1969 film *Medea,* the titular character makes an ominous proclamation: "Niente è più possibile, ormai" (Nothing is possible anymore). Her skepticism – which results from physical and spiritual exile – would be dogmatic, except that time is always already a kind of failure, an "ormai" that can preclude possibility. Yet her remark also serves as a paradox, suggesting that things are indeed possible, only reflectively so. That she says this directly after murdering her children in an apparent act of revenge on Jason, her husband, also evokes not only the ritualistic practices of her people depicted in the beginning of the film, but also the "Binding of Isaac" in the Hebrew Bible. Thus, as a "knight of faith," Medea doesn't murder her children, but rather sacrifices them to the divine Sun and Earth of her homeland, a final attempt at regaining "possibility" and spiritual reconciliation. We do not find out if Medea achieves contrition before succumbing to fire; however, Nicole Raziya Fong's *OЯACULE* seems to suggest that she would necessarily fail, as her faith – however genuine – is misplaced in the Sun and Earth, i.e., the duplicitous properties of light and its reflections, respectively.

This speculation, however, is not beholden to *OЯACULE* alone; Fong's previous book, *PEЯFACT,* illustrates and augments the confluence of sacrifice, light, and deception in *OЯACULE*. Taken together, they emerge as mutually illustrative, with certain subtle and not-so-subtle indicators (e.g., the use of the Cyrillic letter *ya* in the title) that connote symbiosis – not requiring one another but enabling access to certain aspects of their contents. For instance, *PEЯFACT* invokes blueprints for *OЯACULE*'s architecture in lines such as "If repetition is paced by daylight, this is where the rain begins" (Fong, 16), "There is no meaning, only her words" (34), and "That which retains beauty can have no form" (47). However, to view *PEЯFACT* as the locus for *OЯACULE*'s inception is misleading, since nowhere in either text is meaning bound to a specific object or connection – rather, both emanate from their own "unseen depths." Although relationships here are ephemeral and illusory, both books point to the Sun as a cause of delusion. In *OЯACULE*, the light is "inseparable from life and so becoming the most evocative expression of living" (5), simultaneously life's archetypal mask and – as a double-dealing Janus – the revealer of appearance, which, as a binary of reality, represents a kind of non-existence.

In *OЯACULE*'s prologue, Heroine and Luminous present a reading of Plato's *Theaetetus*, a dialogue that contends (among other things) that one must first reach existence before attaining truth. Heroine, who plays Theaetetus, is referred to as "the explanation" (10); she describes light as a "currency" (8) whose value is the establishment of apparitional edges that allow the carving out of imitative or faux existences, suggesting that truth is inaccessible for the characters. They have been subjected to a "great deception," which Heroine describes as:

> a pigeon on the balcony, outlined in transparency against a brick wall which related the substance of a sequined dress to the sexuality of the wearer in a way which removed any kind of precedent from the gaze's originary signing. (10)

To see is not only to detect light but also to fall victim to its trickery, which refracts the masks it reveals: "every surface is retinal" (44). Appearances eternally recede into collective borders, dreaming each other into parody, as in Ursula K. Le Guin's *The Lathe of Heaven*, where "Everything dreams. The play of form, of being, is the dreaming of substance. Rocks have their dreams, and the Earth changes ..." (Le Guin, 167). This reflexive legibility – in which appearance begets – would suggest solipsism if the system itself weren't decidedly imaginary, a product of the Sun's "originary signing." *OЯACULE*'s Sun is the great deceiver, an iteration of Descartes's "Evil Genius," or the demiurge of the Gnostic tradition Yaldabaoth, or what Mina Loy refers to as a "joke" in *The Blind Man*. Regardless, "Appearance attracts a persuasive light" (57) as marked by shimmering boundaries perpetually folding into and elaborating an ideological conformity; the Sun's "currency" resonates with Mark Fisher's notion of capital in *Capitalist Realism,* which functions as "an abstract parasite, an insatiable vampire and zombie maker ... the zombies it makes are us" (Fisher, 15). Even Luminous acknowledges this villainy, although she, too, is light, "not the only star, but one among many others yet to be named" (103):

> [
> In spectacle –   the news reached me:
>   an agony of filaments edited their limit
> beneath the cold sun, becoming legible as
> exterior   [in the sense that they
> concealed me in defaced proximity, I
> could read appearance   into a defiance
> of extent]]]]   In the sense I could
> not doubt the true secrecy of its decay.
>   This corner of discourse decried ... (73)

As one moves through *OЯACULE,* Luminous grows into the apotheosis of appearance, an articulation of light's history, stubbornly refusing to forget. For this reason, Luminous is identified as "notation" (53) and thus is tied to the Tree of Knowledge and nominalization, among other fallen angels. Those angels are in turn preparing to be catalogued or dreamed into *OЯACULE*'s living walls – composed of the stage, Chorus, and Anti-Chorus – a flickering network in which the characters are unable to escape or change. This system is revealed to be a shapeshifter, particularly in part IV, when the stage in Luminous's dream alters from "a greenhouse" (65) to "divine galleries of / deathless flora [divinities]]]]" (67) to a "delivery room" (68) and continues to mutate thereafter.

Luminous's dreams and memories hold metaphysical and semantic extension, as indicated by gardens and flowers that have "overextended / into a semblance of pure appearance" (57). Her gardens reflect light and hatch matryoshkas, each a private Eden "sprayed differently in colour, its rarity and beauty causing the transformation of garden into cupola" (42), the consequence of which is the infinite multiformity of appearance. Flowers represent the apparent flesh of Eden(s), where light (and Luminous) first fell, and its derivative simulacra. In part V, Luminous sings:

> With a flourish, the flowers appear as I remembered them. The flowers appeared in essence to be the same flowers I had seen before. A certain familiarity, sensation of parallelism, convinced me that these flowers had occurred once before – that this iteration was, in a way, a route and programmable recurrence. (126)

Luminous's song articulates the perennial cycle as a feedback loop, where time is likened to a Möbius strip. Impressions of light linger, and memory (in a sort of antagonistic lock with a linear history composed of events that have ostensibly occurred) becomes a kind of intermittence. What materializes in the world of appearance is ephemeral and can't be remembered, only reflected, as in a mirror. Does Pasolini's Medea remember leading her people in human sacrifice, as presented at the beginning of the film, or does the camera merely show it to her (and to us) as a means to an end?

This isn't to suggest that *OЯACULE* connotes collective amnesia but rather that the light-mask remembers for those who appear by embodying recurring cycles, e.g., the seasons, the rising and setting of the Sun, death and resurrection. As Luminous reveals:

uncontested flesh [your memory
is still my incomplete
dream.]]]

You must know it ... (69)

The characters not only seem to be aware of this snare but are also haunted by it. Heroine comments that "Every impossibility is, in essence, a former sensation" (11) and since "sadness is / my only sensation" (57), sorrow represents a demarcation in the tragedy of the characters' condition, calling to mind the happy expressions of those about to be sacrificed in *Medea*, their naive smiles functioning as an edge against which we may recognize the crude shape of human and spiritual brutality. However, there's an oxymoronic expression of variability in the repeated sensation, as the reappearing memory is never temporally the same: "future might exist in iteration of a past yet to occur" (116), which implies the flaw in Medea's nostalgic hope, i.e., that things *were* possible in a definite past.

As Gertrude Stein reminds us in *The Mother of Us All*: "We cannot retrace our steps, going forward may be the same as going backwards" (Stein, 87) – a sentiment that articulates where the ritual act and faith come into play in *OЯACULE*.

Those who suffer within the "living walls" endure agonies of an archetypal sort. The dead Child, evidently perpetually murdered by Heroine and Maternal Love, is resurrected over and over again in light:

> HEROINE
> What formality do I expect from the universe?
>
> CHILD
> For the sun to manoeuvre between leaves?
>
> *Enter MATERNAL LOVE.*
>
> MATERNAL LOVE
> Where else can I keep you? (44–45)

OЯACULE's network, like the fertility cult of Medea and her people, is fundamentally Persephonean, indicated by the characters' entrapment in a recurring cycle of life and death. By not mentioning Persephone, they follow a social and religious protocol of classical antiquity, as the name was simultaneously feared and respected for its powerful association with death and destruction. For example, Empedocles refers to Persephone euphemistically as Nestis, "who moistens the springs of men with her tears," the divine embodiment of the element water. Persephone resurrects with rain and suffering, a terrifying possibility for the characters, as she may very well be the one who announces:

> *I am such as spring in recurrence relates its abhorrent position.*
> *I am such as the decaying remnants of illusion invoke their relative excess.* (54)

Persephonean worship is the adulation of spring, the categorical expression of cyclic reflections from which one can't withdraw. Spring is also a form of recollection reminiscent of Rousseau's conception of the cultivation of grain as a recurring wellspring of corruption, a Sisyphean evil. Any motion in *OЯACULE* feels like a recurrent deception, the cinematic illusion of frames shown in quick succession to give the impression of movement. For instance, the Anti-Chorus chant "Repeat, Repeal, Return, Repeal, Recede, Repeat, Repeat, Renew ..." (42) and order the characters to adhere to the network; this in turn correlates to Zeno's dichotomy paradox, which was described by Aristotle as "assert[ing] the non-existence of motion on the ground that that which is in locomotion must arrive at the halfway stage before it arrives at the goal" (Kinsey, 9). Any hope for a break in the perennial cycle first requires faith in a kind of "Fifth Season" (as per Albucius's conception of that which repeats beyond the traditional seasons), a vanishing point beyond "dawn's circuitous element / (beyond dawn's elemental radiance)" (123).

OЯACULE not only orders us to disappear but to "vanish differently" (19) from the feedback loop, perhaps as Issa Samb commands we do in "Musée Dynamique": "Enfonce le rideau. Brûle ta mémoire" (Samb, 321) (Rip down the curtain. Burn your memory). The characters suggest that there's a "dislocation," which is described by Luminous as "a circumstantial room at the core of a disappearance" (120), although Maternal Love tells us that to inhabit the room is a "mythic feat, perhaps existing only in lore" (49). Perhaps the Fifth Season is the natural result of the eternal recurrence of the cycle, in which Sisyphean entanglement is a perpetual motion that bores down on itself for so long that it wears out its network and becomes the vanishing point. After all, the cycle is both a "repeating, / ... continuing and failing to" (99), suggesting a predetermined gap elsewhere, a portal to an unknown place. But can we trust Luminous, who like Pasolini's Chiron the centaur, is a great liar by admission? All possibility of escape is speculation. However, the "explanation" warns us not to "try to establish me in the midst of my indifference" (14).

Again, "*The essence of this indifference is multiple*" (90); the indifference is not an endgame, and neither is its echoing. Though we're reflections of light, light arises from within us as well. Perhaps, then, we vanish when we go beyond our own "elemental radiance," privileging others over ourselves. We mustn't dismiss the potential of self-abnegation. It's a good place to start.

WORKS CITED

Fisher, Mark. *Capitalist Realism: Is There No Alternative?* Winchester, UK: Zero Books, 2009.

Fong, Nicole Raziya. *PEЯFACT*. Vancouver, BC: Talonbooks, 2019.

Kinsey, L. Christine, Teresa E. Moore, and Stratos Prassidis. *Geometry and Symmetry*. Hoboken, NJ: John Wiley and Sons, 2010.

Le Guin, Ursula K. *The Lathe of Heaven*. New York: Simon and Schuster, (1971) 2008.

Loy, Mina. "In … Formation." *Blind Man* 1 (April 10, 1917).

Samb, Issa. "Musée Dynamique." In *Word! Word? Word! Issa Samb and the Undecipherable Form*, edited by Koyo Kouoh, 218–347. Berlin: Sternberg Press, 2013.

Stein, Gertrude. "The Mother of Us All." In *Last Opera and Plays*, edited by Carl Van Vechten, 52–88. Baltimore: Johns Hopkins University Press, 1995.

ACKNOWLEDGMENTS

Thank you, Talonbooks, for believing in this project and bringing it into the immediate world. Special thanks to Catriona Strang, Kevin Williams, and Leslie Smith.

Thank you, Andy Martrich, for your incredible insight, attention, and care taken with *OЯACULE*.

To those whose work within poetry has been directive, without whose support and friendship I surely would be at a loss: Erín Moure, Kaie Kellough, Michael Nardone, Mark Francis Johnson, Nathan Brown, and rob mclennan.

Thank you, Nora.
Thank you, Sirius (the most ineffable star).

Thank you, Cynthia Mitchell, Georgia Phillips-Amos, Jesse Ruddock, Nico, Uma Nardone, Stephanie E. Creaghan, Tanisha Arthur, and the "Laceration Reading Group."

Earlier versions of work within *OЯACULE* have appeared in *filling Station, Social Text, Touch the Donkey, DUSIE, Some, carte blanche,* and *RECOMMENDER ENGINE*. Thanks to the editors.

Nicole Raziya Fong is a poet living in Tiohtià:ke/Montréal, Québec. Her previous book, *PEЯFACT* (Talonbooks, 2019), aimed to coax the immateriality of psychic experience into embodying a muscular, acting physique. Her poetic work invokes a subject within multiplicity, fragmenting time and identity onto a responsive, echoic field. Her writing has appeared in various publications including *Social Text, Cordite Poetry Review, carte blanche,* the *Capilano Review* and the *Volta,* and has been translated into Swedish and French.

PHOTO: Nora Fulton